PREFACE

INTRODUCTION

CHAPTER 1: CRAFTING A COMPELLING VISION AND PURPOSE STATEMENT

CHAPTER 2: LEADERSHIP ANCHORED IN ETHICS AND INTEGRITY

CHAPTER 3: IN-DEPTH EXPLORATION OF ESG PRINCIPLES

CHAPTER 4: THE ENVIRONMENTAL DIMENSION: LEADING SUSTAINABLE CHANGE

CHAPTER 5: SOCIAL RESPONSIBILITY: CULTIVATING INCLUSIVITY AND WELL-BEING

CHAPTER 6: GOVERNANCE FOR THE FUTURE: ETHICAL STRUCTURES AND ACCOUNTABILITY

CHAPTER 7: RESILIENCE IN LEADERSHIP: NAVIGATING CHALLENGES WITH PURPOSE

CHAPTER 8: MAPPING YOUR IMPACT: UNDERSTANDING AND APPLYING MATERIALITY

CHAPTER 9: FRAMEWORKS FOR PURPOSE-DRIVEN LEADERSHIP

CHAPTER 10: COMMUNICATING YOUR ESG JOURNEY

CHAPTER 11: LEADING WITH PURPOSE: TRANSFORMING CHALLENGES INTO OPPORTUNITIES

CHAPTER 12: ENVISIONING THE FUTURE OF PURPOSE-DRIVEN LEADERSHIP

Preface

In today's rapidly evolving world, the landscape of leadership is undergoing a profound transformation. Gone are the days when success was solely measured by profit margins and market share. The leaders of tomorrow face a new set of challenges, as well as opportunities, defined by the urgent need for sustainability, social equity, and ethical governance. It is against this backdrop that "Purpose at the Helm: Mastering ESG Leadership for the Future" was conceived.

This book is born out of a conviction that the role of a leader in the 21st century is not just to navigate the complexities of the business world but to do so with a deep sense of purpose and a commitment to the greater good. The challenges of climate change, social inequality, and corporate governance demand a new breed of leaders—leaders who are as passionate about making a positive impact on the world as they are about achieving business success. Our journey begins with a simple yet profound question: What does it mean to lead with purpose in today's world? To answer this, we delve into the principles of Environmental, Social, and Governance (ESG) and explore how they can be integrated with purpose-driven leadership to create organizations that are not only successful but also sustainable and ethical.

The imperative for purpose-driven leadership in the modern business landscape has never been more critical. In a world marked by rapid environmental changes, social upheavals, and evolving expectations of corporate governance, the call for leaders who can navigate these complexities with a clear sense of purpose and ethical direction is loud and clear. Purpose-driven leadership transcends the traditional focus on financial metrics, encompassing a broader vision that integrates the well-being of communities, the planet, and sustainable business practices. Societal expectations of businesses have shifted dramatically. Consumers, employees, and stakeholders now demand transparency, ethical practices, and a genuine commitment to social and environmental issues. Leaders are expected to not only understand these expectations but to actively align their organization's strategies and operations to meet them.

With climate change posing an existential threat to the planet, businesses are under increasing pressure to mitigate their environmental impact. Purpose-driven leaders recognize the urgency of this challenge and are at the forefront of adopting sustainable practices, not just as a compliance measure, but as a core aspect of their business model.

The rise of social movements and a growing awareness of inequality have amplified the need for leaders to champion diversity, equity, and inclusion within their organizations. Purpose-driven leadership involves creating opportunities, fostering a culture of respect and belonging, and ensuring that all voices are heard and valued. In an era where corporate scandals can quickly erode public trust, ethical governance has become a cornerstone of purpose-driven leadership. This means not only adhering to laws and regulations but setting higher standards for accountability, transparency, and integrity within the organization.

The imperative for purpose-driven leadership is about redefining success. It's about leaders who understand that their organization's long-term viability is intrinsically linked to their ability to generate positive social and environmental outcomes alongside financial profits. This holistic approach to leadership is essential for navigating the complexities of the modern business landscape and for building organizations that thrive by making a meaningful impact on the world. The imperative for purpose-driven leadership is clear. It calls for leaders who are visionary, empathetic, resilient, and unwavering in their commitment to driving change. As we look to the future, the success of businesses and the well-being of our planet depend on leaders who are willing to put purpose at the helm.

The goal of this book is not to provide a one-size-fits-all blueprint for leadership. Rather, it is to inspire current and future leaders to think deeply about their own leadership philosophy and how it can be shaped by the principles of purpose and ESG. Through frameworks, practical insights, real-world exercises, and strategies for resilience and impact, we aim to equip leaders with the tools they need to lead with integrity, navigate the challenges of our time, and make a lasting positive impact on the world.

"Purpose at the Helm" is an invitation to embark on a transformative leadership journey. It is a journey that requires courage, vision, and a steadfast commitment to values that extend beyond the boardroom. As you turn these pages, I hope you find inspiration, insight, and, above all, a renewed sense of purpose in your role as a leader.

Welcome to the future of leadership.

Introduction

In the unfolding narrative of the 21st century, the global landscape presents an intricate tapestry of challenges and opportunities. From the escalating climate crisis and widening social inequalities to the urgent calls for transparent and accountable governance, the complexities of our times demand more than just conventional leadership. It is within this context that the concepts of purpose-driven leadership and Environmental, Social, and Governance (ESG) principles emerge not just as responses, but as essential strategies for navigating the uncertainties of our era.

This introduction seeks to illuminate the pivotal role that purpose-driven leadership, underscored by robust ESG practices, plays in steering organizations and societies towards sustainable futures. In doing so, it underscores the critical need for leaders who can transcend traditional paradigms to address the multifaceted challenges of our time. As the expectations from businesses and leaders evolve against a backdrop of global challenges, the call for a new breed of leadership has become increasingly apparent. Today's leaders are expected not only to drive financial success but to do so with a clear sense of purpose and responsibility towards the planet and its people. Purpose-driven leadership, therefore, emerges as a beacon of hope and direction, offering a pathway to navigate through the storms of uncertainty.

Purpose-driven leaders are distinguished by their unwavering commitment to a vision that extends beyond profit maximization to include social betterment and environmental stewardship. This form of leadership is not just about setting and achieving goals but about imbuing every decision and action with a sense of purpose that resonates with stakeholders at all levels. In an era marked by rapid changes and unpredictability, the role of purpose in providing direction, motivation, and resilience cannot be overstated.

By anchoring their strategies and operations in purpose, leaders can inspire their organizations to adapt, innovate, and thrive, even in the face of adversity. Purpose acts as a compass that guides organizations through turbulent times, ensuring that they remain focused on their core values and objectives. Moreover, it fosters a culture of engagement and loyalty among employees, customers, and other stakeholders, who are increasingly seeking to align themselves with organizations that reflect their values and aspirations. The evolving expectations from businesses and their leaders signify a profound shift towards more ethical, sustainable, and socially responsible practices. In this new paradigm, purpose-driven leadership becomes not just desirable but essential. Leaders who embrace this approach find themselves better equipped to navigate the complexities of the modern world, transforming challenges into opportunities for growth, innovation, and positive impact.

As we delve deeper into the intricacies of purpose-driven leadership and ESG principles, it becomes clear that these are not merely trends but fundamental shifts in the way businesses operate and lead. The following chapters will explore the various dimensions of this transformative approach to leadership, offering insights, strategies, and practical guidance for those ready to embark on this journey.

In today's world, where the impact of businesses extends well beyond their financial performance, the Environmental, Social, and Governance (ESG) framework stands as a critical measure of a company's sustainability and ethical impact. ESG represents a holistic approach to assessing a company's operations and policies in terms of their environmental stewardship, social responsibility, and governance standards. This framework is increasingly recognized not just for its ethical implications but also for its direct correlation with long-term business success and resilience.

- Environmental considerations focus on a company's ecological impact. This includes how it manages resources, reduces emissions, and contributes to the preservation of natural habitats. In the face of climate change, businesses are expected to play a pivotal role in driving environmental sustainability.

- Social factors assess how a company manages relationships with employees, suppliers, customers, and communities. It encompasses issues such as labor practices, product responsibility, and community engagement. In an era where social issues are at the forefront of public consciousness, a company's commitment to social well-being is crucial for attracting and retaining talent, customers, and investors.

- Governance involves the structures and practices that govern the organization's management and oversight. This includes board diversity, executive pay, corruption, and transparency. Strong governance practices ensure accountability and align the interests of management with those of shareholders and other stakeholders.

The integration of ESG principles into business operations and strategy is proving to be a key differentiator in the marketplace. Companies that excel in ESG are not only mitigating risks but are also leveraging opportunities for innovation, enhancing their reputation, and building trust with stakeholders. As such, ESG is not merely a compliance or ethical checklist but a strategic framework that drives sustainable business practices, resilience, and long-term value creation.

This book is designed with the ambitious goal of equipping current and aspiring leaders with the knowledge, skills, and mindset necessary to navigate the complex interplay between purpose-driven leadership and ESG principles. By integrating these elements into their leadership practices, leaders can steer their organizations towards sustainable success, creating a positive ripple effect across their stakeholders and society at large.

The objectives of this book are twofold:

1. To offer a comprehensive guide on integrating purpose and ESG principles into leadership practices: Through exploring

the nuances of ESG and purpose-driven leadership, this book aims to provide leaders with a robust framework for understanding and applying these principles in their organizations. This includes practical insights, strategic advice, and real-world examples that demonstrate the transformative power of aligning business operations with ethical, environmental, and social values.

2. To equip leaders with the knowledge, skills, and mindset necessary for creating positive change: Beyond understanding the "what" and "why" of ESG and purpose-driven leadership, this book seeks to empower leaders with the "how." Through exercises, case studies, and reflective questions, readers will develop the capabilities to implement these principles in their leadership approach, driving meaningful change within their organizations and contributing to a more sustainable and equitable world.

As we delve deeper into the subsequent chapters, readers will embark on a journey of discovery, learning how to effectively blend purpose and ESG principles into a cohesive leadership strategy. This journey promises not only to enhance the leader's impact on their organization but also to contribute to the broader goal of shaping a more sustainable, just, and prosperous future for all. This explorative journey through "Purpose at the Helm: Mastering ESG Leadership for the Future," prepares you to dive deep into the realms of purpose-driven leadership and the Environmental, Social, and Governance (ESG) principles that are reshaping the business world. This book is structured to not only enlighten but also to equip you with the practical tools and insights needed to navigate the complexities of contemporary leadership.

The book unfolds in a carefully curated sequence of chapters, each dedicated to a pivotal aspect of purpose-driven leadership and ESG integration. Beginning with the foundational concepts of purpose and ESG, the narrative progresses to delve into specific strategies for embedding these principles into your leadership practice. Through a blend of theoretical frameworks, real-world case studies, and interactive exercises, the book offers a comprehensive guide to understanding and applying purpose-driven leadership and ESG in various organizational contexts.

Key areas covered include:

- Crafting compelling vision and purpose statements to guide organizational direction.

- Embedding ethics and integrity within the leadership fabric of the organization.

- Navigating the environmental dimension of leadership, focusing on sustainability and stewardship.

- Cultivating inclusivity and well-being through social responsibility initiatives.

- Strengthening organizational governance with ethical structures and accountability.

- Building resilience to navigate challenges with purpose and adaptability.

- Mapping your impact through understanding and applying materiality in ESG.

- Communicating your ESG journey effectively to engage and inspire stakeholders.

Each chapter is designed to build upon the previous, creating a layered understanding of how purpose-driven leadership and ESG principles intersect and how they can be harnessed to drive meaningful change. Within these pages, you will encounter a variety of frameworks that offer structured approaches to integrating purpose and ESG into your leadership. These frameworks serve as blueprints, guiding your strategic thinking and decision-making processes.

Real-world case studies provide a window into how other leaders and organizations have navigated the challenges and opportunities of purpose-driven leadership and ESG. These narratives are chosen for their diversity, showcasing a wide range of industries, geographies, and organizational sizes. Through these stories, you will gain insights into practical applications, potential pitfalls, and innovative solutions.

Interactive exercises are woven throughout the book, inviting you to apply what you've learned to your own context. These activities range from crafting vision and purpose statements to conducting materiality assessments and developing ESG reporting outlines. Each exercise is designed to deepen your understanding and enhance your ability to implement purpose-driven leadership and ESG principles in a meaningful way.

Strategies for overcoming common obstacles and leading transformative change provide you with actionable guidance. These strategies draw on best practices and lessons learned from both successes and failures, offering you a robust toolkit for leading with purpose and ESG.

This book is a call to action for current and aspiring leaders to embrace the journey of becoming purpose-driven, ESG-integrated leaders. The path ahead requires more than traditional leadership skills; it demands a commitment to continuous learning, ethical decision-making, and the cultivation of a strategic vision that encompasses not just the welfare of the organization but also that of society and the environment.

Continuous learning is fundamental in this rapidly evolving landscape. As ESG standards, societal expectations, and environmental challenges shift, so too must your knowledge and strategies. This book provides a foundation, but true mastery comes from staying informed, seeking out new information, and being open to evolving your approach.

Ethical decision-making is at the heart of purpose-driven leadership. It involves choosing paths that align with your core values and the broader good, even when faced with tough decisions or potential trade-offs. This book aims to strengthen your ethical compass and provide you with the tools to navigate these complex decisions with integrity.

Strategic vision, grounded in purpose and informed by ESG principles, enables you to lead with foresight and adaptability. It involves not only envisioning a sustainable future but also mapping out the practical steps to achieve it. Through the insights and exercises provided, you will be encouraged to develop and refine your strategic vision, aligning it with the principles of purpose-driven leadership and ESG. As you turn each page, remember that the journey to becoming a purpose-driven leader is both personal and collective. It is a journey of growth, challenge, and profound reward. Armed with the knowledge, skills, and mindset fostered by this book, you are poised to make a significant impact on your organization, society, and the environment. Welcome to the future of leadership.

As we stand at the threshold of a new era in leadership, the call to lead with purpose and to integrate Environmental, Social, and Governance (ESG) principles into the core of our leadership practices has never been more pressing. The challenges of our time demand leaders who are not only adept at navigating the complexities of the business world but who are also committed to making a positive impact on society and the environment. This book has been crafted with the intention of equipping you, the reader, with the knowledge, strategies, and insights necessary to answer this call.

Remember that leading with purpose is about more than just adopting a set of principles; it's about embodying a vision for a better world and taking actionable steps to bring that vision to life through your leadership. It is about inspiring those around you to join in a collective effort to drive meaningful change. This book serves as your guide, offering a comprehensive exploration of purpose-driven leadership and ESG, enriched with frameworks, case studies, exercises, and strategies designed to empower you to lead with integrity, resilience, and vision.

We urge you to embrace the call to lead with purpose. Let the insights and resources provided in this book serve as a foundation upon which you can build your approach to leadership—one that not only achieves organizational success but also contributes to a more sustainable, equitable, and thriving world. The journey of purpose-driven leadership is both a privilege and a responsibility, one that holds the promise of transforming challenges into opportunities for impact.

This book sets the stage for a transformative exploration into the depths of purpose-driven leadership and ESG. It is an invitation to embark on a journey that will not only challenge and inspire you but also prepare you to meet the demands and embrace the opportunities of the modern business world with confidence and foresight. As you turn each page, remember that the future of leadership is in your hands, and the impact you make through your leadership can leave a lasting legacy for generations to come. Let's lead the way forward, together.

Chapter 1: Crafting a Compelling Vision and Purpose Statement

In the journey of leadership and organizational development, few tools are as foundational yet profoundly impactful as the crafting of vision and purpose statements. These statements do more than just adorn the walls of your office or the front page of your website; they serve as the north star for every strategic decision, guiding the direction and ethos of the organization.

Vision statements articulate a future-oriented, aspirational goal of what an organization aims to achieve in the long term. It is the destination on the organizational map, providing a clear direction for where the company is headed. Purpose statements, on the other hand, answer the fundamental question of "why" the organization exists beyond making a profit. It delves into the organization's core reason for being, reflecting its values, ethos, and the impact it seeks to have on the world.

The distinction between vision and purpose statements is critical, yet they are intrinsically connected. While the vision provides a concrete goal, the purpose offers the motivation and framework within which that goal is pursued. Together, they form a cohesive narrative that inspires action, guides decision-making, and shapes the organizational culture.

At the heart of every remarkable organization lies a clearly defined purpose. This is not merely a statement of intent but a reflection of the core values and beliefs that drive the organization. Identifying and articulating this purpose requires introspection, dialogue, and a deep understanding of the organization's unique impact on its stakeholders and the wider community.

1. Understanding Core Values and Beliefs: The process begins with identifying the core values and beliefs that define the organization. These are the non-negotiable principles that guide its actions and decisions. Engaging with employees, customers, and other stakeholders can provide valuable insights into what these values are and how they are perceived.

2. Strategies for Articulating Purpose: Once the core values are identified, the next step is to articulate a purpose that resonates. This involves translating these values into a compelling narrative that connects with stakeholders on an emotional level. It's about telling a story that explains not just what the organization does, but why it matters.

3. The Role of Purpose in Inspiring Action: A well-defined purpose statement becomes a powerful tool for inspiring action and guiding decision-making across the organization. It ensures that every strategy, every project, and every initiative aligns with the broader goals and values of the organization. Purpose acts as a rallying cry, motivating employees, attracting customers, and engaging partners in a shared mission.

Crafting compelling vision and purpose statements is more than an exercise in branding or marketing. It is a foundational step in building an organization that is resilient, adaptive, and capable of making a significant impact. As leaders embark on this process, they unlock the potential to transform their organization's trajectory, culture, and ultimately, its legacy. This chapter will guide you through understanding, defining, and articulating your organization's vision and purpose, laying the groundwork for a journey of purpose-driven leadership.

An effective vision statement serves as a beacon, guiding the organization towards a defined future. It possesses certain characteristics that make it both inspiring and actionable:

- Clarity: It articulates a clear and concise picture of the future, understandable to all stakeholders.

- Aspirational: It reaches beyond the current state, setting an ambitious goal that motivates and inspires.

- Aligns with Purpose and Values: It reflects the organization's core values and its overarching purpose, ensuring consistency in direction.

- Future-focused: It looks ahead, projecting a long-term vision for what the organization aims to achieve.

- Achievable: While aspirational, it remains grounded in reality, suggesting a future that, though challenging, is attainable.

Steps to Envisioning a Future That Aligns with the Organization's Purpose and Values

1. Reflect on Core Values and Purpose: Begin by revisiting the organization's core values and purpose. These elements should serve as the foundation of your vision.

2. Engage Stakeholders: Involve employees, customers, and other key stakeholders in discussions about their hopes and aspirations for the organization's future. Their insights can provide valuable perspectives that enrich the vision.

3. Identify Key Themes: From these discussions, identify recurring themes or ideas that resonate strongly with the organization's goals and values.

4. Project into the Future: Imagine the organization several years down the line, considering the impact of potential global, industry, and societal changes. How does your organization evolve in response?

5. Draft the Vision Statement: Using the insights gathered, draft a statement that encapsulates the envisioned future, ensuring it embodies the identified characteristics of an effective vision statement.

Techniques for Creating a Clear, Compelling, and Achievable Vision

- Use Vivid Imagery: Employ language that paints a vivid picture of the future, making the vision tangible and relatable.

- Incorporate Emotive Language: Utilize words that evoke emotion and passion, connecting on a deeper level with stakeholders.

- Simplicity is Key: Avoid jargon and complex language. The vision should be easily understood by everyone.

- Iterate and Refine: A vision statement can evolve. Don't hesitate to refine it over time as the organization and its context change.

The journey from crafting to implementing an organization's vision and purpose is pivotal. It transforms lofty ideals into tangible practices that shape the everyday operations and culture of the organization. Leaders play a crucial role in this process, not only by embedding these principles into the organizational fabric but also by embodying them in their leadership.

Embedding an organization's vision and purpose into its daily operations begins with clear communication. Leaders must ensure that every member of the organization understands these guiding principles and sees how they relate to their specific roles and responsibilities. This clarity helps individuals connect their day-to-day activities with the broader organizational goals, fostering a sense of contribution and purpose.

Leading by example is perhaps the most powerful strategy for inspiring alignment with the organization's vision and purpose. When leaders consistently demonstrate their commitment to these principles through their decisions, actions, and interactions, they set a standard for others to follow. This embodiment of the vision and purpose serves as a living testament to their importance, motivating others to integrate these values into their own work and behavior.

Inspiring others requires leaders to recognize and celebrate instances where employees' actions align with the organization's vision and purpose. Acknowledgment and appreciation reinforce the significance of these principles and encourage their continued adoption throughout the organization.

The implementation of vision and purpose is not a one-time effort but an ongoing process that requires leaders to be adaptable and responsive to changing circumstances. The external environment, including market trends, societal expectations, and technological advancements, is always evolving. Similarly, the internal dynamics of an organization—such as its goals, challenges, and team composition—can shift over time. These changes necessitate a periodic review of the organization's vision and purpose statements to ensure they remain relevant and resonant.

Leaders should facilitate regular discussions about the organization's direction and values, inviting feedback from across the organization. This collaborative approach not only helps in identifying when updates to the vision and purpose might be needed but also strengthens the collective ownership of these principles. Revisiting and refining the organization's guiding statements becomes a strategic exercise in ensuring their continued alignment with both internal aspirations and external realities.

The effective implementation of an organization's vision and purpose into its leadership practices and operations is a dynamic and continuous process. It requires clear communication, leading by example, fostering a culture of recognition, and remaining open to adaptation. By navigating this process thoughtfully, leaders can ensure that their organization's vision and purpose are not just words on a page but are living, breathing forces driving the organization forward.

Case Study: Patagonia - A Testament to Vision and Purpose
Introduction

Patagonia stands as a leading figure in the outdoor apparel industry, renowned not just for its products but for its unwavering dedication to environmental activism and corporate responsibility. Founded by Yvon Chouinard in 1973, the company has set itself apart with a clear mission: to save our home planet. This case study delves into how Patagonia's commitment to its vision and purpose has propelled its success, the strategies for embodying these ideals, and the lessons gleaned from overcoming inherent challenges.

At the heart of Patagonia's ethos is a vision that transcends conventional business goals — "We're in business to save our home planet." This vision is supported by a purpose deeply embedded in environmental activism and sustainable practices. Every aspect of the company's operation, from product design to supply chain management, is influenced by its quest to mitigate environmental impact.

Patagonia manifests its dedication to its core values through various initiatives. The company prioritizes the use of organic cotton and recycled materials to minimize environmental harm. Through its "1% for the Planet" program, it contributes to environmental campaigns and projects worldwide. Moreover, Patagonia has engaged in corporate activism, taking stands on issues such as the protection of national monuments and climate change advocacy.

Transparency and impact define Patagonia's communication approach. Utilizing its website, social media platforms, and documentary films, the company advocates for environmental conservation and shares stories of activism. Its marketing campaigns often spotlight environmental issues, reinforcing its commitment over promoting its products.

Despite its achievements, Patagonia navigates challenges such as the complexities of maintaining a sustainable supply chain and the paradox of advocating for the planet while operating in a consumer-driven industry. The company tackles these issues by striving to reduce its environmental footprint, encouraging the repair and reuse of its products, and maintaining transparency about its sustainability journey.

The journey of Patagonia emphasizes the significance of authenticity in embodying a vision and purpose. The company has cultivated trust among its stakeholders by being candid about its challenges and progress. This commitment to purpose has spurred innovation, leading to the development of sustainable materials and new forms of environmental activism. Patagonia's story illustrates that activism and profitability can coexist, demonstrating that businesses can serve as powerful agents of positive change.

Patagonia's narrative showcases the transformative potential of aligning a company with a strong vision and purpose. By steadfastly adhering to its values, Patagonia has not only enjoyed commercial success but has also made significant contributions to environmental conservation. The company stands as an exemplar for others, proving that a deep commitment to vision and purpose can navigate and overcome significant challenges, affirming that business can indeed be a force for good in the world.

Guided Exercise to Explore and Define Personal and Organizational Values

Objective: Identify and articulate the core values driving your leadership and organizational culture.

Materials Needed: Notepads, pens, flip charts or whiteboard, sticky notes.

Instructions

1. Individual Reflection: Each participant writes down 3-5 values they believe are at the core of their personal leadership style and their organization's culture. For each value, participants should note a specific instance where this value influenced a decision or action in their professional life.

2. Group Discussion: Form small groups of 4-5 participants. Each person shares their listed values and the examples of how these values are manifested. The group discusses these values, focusing on similarities, differences, and any new insights that emerge.

3. Feedback Session: Groups select the most resonant values and present them to the class. Encourage feedback from other groups and instructors to explore alignment between personal and organizational values and the impact of these values on leadership effectiveness.

Step-by-Step Activity to Draft a Purpose Statement

Objective: Craft a concise statement that captures the essence of your organization's purpose beyond profit.

Materials Needed: Worksheet with guiding questions, pens.

Individual Work: Participants answer guided questions on a worksheet:

- "Why does our organization exist beyond making a profit?"
- "What impact does our organization aim to have on its customers, employees, and community?"

Pair and Share: In pairs, participants share their responses and discuss the underlying themes that emerge. This discussion helps refine thoughts and articulate a more cohesive purpose.

Drafting the Purpose Statement: Using insights from the discussion, each participant drafts a purpose statement for their organization. Aim for clarity and succinctness, capturing the organization's reason for being in no more than three sentences.

Group Review: Share drafted purpose statements within small groups and provide constructive feedback to refine and strengthen the statements.

Develop a Vision Statement

Objective: Create a vision statement that outlines the future aspirations for your organization.

Materials Needed: Vision statement worksheet, pens, large sheets of paper for brainstorming, markers.

Instructions

Brainstorming Session: In groups, participants brainstorm answers to the following:

- "Based on our defined purpose and values, what do we aim to achieve in the future?"

- "What does success look like in 5, 10, or 20 years? Be specific about milestones or achievements."

Drafting the Vision Statement: Each group uses the brainstormed ideas to draft a vision statement that encapsulates their aspirations for the organization. The statement should be forward-looking, inspiring, and aligned with the organization's purpose and values.

Presentation and Feedback: Groups present their vision statements to the class. Collect feedback from other participants and instructors, focusing on the clarity, aspiration, and alignment of the vision statement with the organization's purpose and values.
Refinement: Based on feedback, each group refines their vision statement. The goal is to arrive at a clear, compelling, and achievable vision for the future.

These interactive exercises are designed to engage participants actively in the process of defining their personal and organizational values, crafting a purpose statement, and envisioning a future through a clear vision statement. Through reflection, discussion, and collaborative feedback, participants will leave with foundational statements that not only guide their leadership and organizational direction but also serve to inspire and mobilize their teams towards a shared and vibrant future.

Chapter 2: Leadership Anchored in Ethics and Integrity

In the realm of leadership, few qualities are as universally esteemed as ethics and integrity. These principles are not merely desirable attributes but the very foundation upon which effective, impactful leadership is built. In a world increasingly defined by complexity and change, the indispensability of ethics and integrity in leadership becomes even more pronounced. For organizations driven by a purpose beyond profit, ethical leadership is not optional; it is essential.

Ethical leadership serves as the cornerstone for organizations aiming to navigate the challenges of the modern business environment with honor and responsibility. It involves making decisions that are not only legally compliant but also morally sound, reflecting a deep commitment to doing what is right, irrespective of the circumstances. This chapter delves into the critical importance of ethics and integrity, illustrating how they are vital for fostering cultures of trust, accountability, and mutual respect within organizations.

At its core, ethical leadership influences every aspect of organizational life. From internal decision-making processes to external interactions with stakeholders, the ethical stance taken by leaders shapes the organizational culture, affecting how trust is built and maintained. When leaders consistently demonstrate ethical behavior, they set a standard that encourages similar conduct throughout the organization. This alignment between stated values and actual practices reinforces stakeholder trust, an invaluable asset in today's business landscape.

Committing to ethical leadership is not without its challenges. Leaders often face situations where the right course of action is not clear-cut, where competing interests must be balanced, and where short-term pressures might tempt a compromise on long-held values. These scenarios test the resilience of ethical commitments, presenting both challenges and opportunities for growth.

Upholding ethics and integrity requires a deliberate, thoughtful approach. Leaders must be equipped to navigate ethical dilemmas, making decisions that reflect their organization's core values and purpose. This involves cultivating an environment where ethical considerations are part of every conversation, where employees feel empowered to speak up about concerns, and where integrity is both expected and rewarded.

The impact of ethical leadership extends beyond the internal workings of an organization. In a broader context, organizations led by ethical principles contribute positively to their industries and communities. They become beacons of trust and integrity, attracting customers, partners, and employees who share similar values. This alignment between organizational practices and societal expectations amplifies the organization's influence, driving meaningful change in the world.

The journey of ethical leadership is continuous, demanding vigilance, courage, and an unwavering commitment to principle. As we explore the nuances of ethical leadership further, we will uncover strategies for embedding ethics and integrity into the fabric of organizational leadership, ensuring that these foundational principles guide leaders in their quest to lead purpose-driven organizations towards sustainable success.

In the complex landscape of modern leadership, ethical frameworks serve as invaluable tools, guiding leaders through the labyrinth of moral dilemmas they encounter. These frameworks provide structured approaches to evaluating situations, ensuring that decisions are made with a consistent and principled basis.

One such framework is the **Principles-based Approach,** which relies on universal ethical principles such as justice, autonomy, and beneficence. Leaders who employ this approach weigh their decisions against these fundamental principles, striving to act in ways that uphold them.

Another framework is the **Consequences-based Approach,** often associated with utilitarianism, which evaluates the ethicality of actions based on their outcomes. Decisions made under this framework aim to maximize positive outcomes or benefits for the greatest number of people.

The **Virtue Ethics Approach** focuses on the character of the decision-maker rather than the act itself or its consequences. It emphasizes moral virtues such as honesty, courage, and compassion, guiding leaders to act in ways that embody these qualities.

Applying these frameworks in everyday leadership practice involves a deliberate process of reflection and analysis. Leaders must first identify the ethical dimensions of a situation, then evaluate their options through the lens of their chosen ethical framework. This process not only aids in making sound moral decisions but also in explaining and defending these decisions to others within the organization.

Maintaining integrity in the face of challenges, temptations, or crises is a hallmark of ethical leadership. This often requires courage and resilience, as well as a deep commitment to one's values and principles.

Strategies for preserving integrity under pressure include clear communication of ethical standards within the organization, creating an environment where ethical behavior is expected and supported. Building a strong support network of peers and mentors who share a commitment to ethical principles can provide crucial backing in difficult times.

Ethical leadership development programs can equip leaders with the skills and insights needed to navigate ethical challenges effectively. These programs often include training on ethical decision-making frameworks, as well as techniques for ethical problem-solving and conflict resolution.

When faced with ethical challenges, leaders must navigate the complexities with a clear commitment to their core values and the overarching purpose of their organization. Developing responses that align with these foundational principles requires a thoughtful approach, blending wisdom with integrity. A crucial aspect of this process involves ensuring that decisions not only adhere to ethical standards but also resonate with the mission and vision of the organization. This alignment reinforces the authenticity of the leadership and the ethical stance of the organization as a whole.

Transparency, accountability, and communication emerge as pivotal elements in the realm of ethical leadership. Transparency involves being open about the decision-making process, sharing the rationale behind decisions, and the implications they hold for the organization and its stakeholders. This openness fosters trust and respect, setting a standard for honesty within the organization.

Accountability is equally critical, with leaders taking responsibility for their decisions and the outcomes they produce. This includes acknowledging mistakes and taking corrective action when necessary, demonstrating a commitment to ethical integrity even in the face of adversity.

Effective communication acts as the bridge that connects leaders with their teams, stakeholders, and the broader community. Communicating ethical decisions and the values driving them helps build a shared understanding and alignment within the organization. This shared sense of purpose is essential for navigating ethical challenges collectively and maintaining organizational integrity.

Ethical courage stands as a beacon for leaders dedicated to enacting change and maintaining high standards within their organizations. This form of courage is about standing firm in one's convictions, especially when faced with situations that test one's principles. It involves making tough decisions that may not be popular or may come with personal and professional risks, but are in line with ethical principles and the greater good.

Stories of leaders who have exhibited ethical courage serve as powerful illustrations of its impact. Consider a leader who, despite potential backlash, chose to publicly address and rectify unethical practices within their organization. By doing so, not only did they reaffirm the organization's commitment to ethical conduct, but they also set a precedent for transparency and accountability that strengthened the organization's reputation and trust with stakeholders. Another example involves a leader who took a stand against industry norms that conflicted with environmental sustainability, opting instead for practices that favored long-term ecological health over short-term profits. This decision not only demonstrated a commitment to environmental stewardship but also inspired innovation within the organization, leading to sustainable solutions that benefited both the company and the planet.

These stories highlight the transformative power of ethical courage. By choosing to lead with integrity and courage, leaders not only uphold their own ethical standards but also inspire those around them to do the same. The ripple effect of such leadership can lead to significant positive changes within organizations and society at large, showcasing the profound impact ethical courage can have on the world.

As we conclude this exploration into the vital role of ethics and integrity in purpose-driven leadership, several key takeaways crystallize. These principles are not mere embellishments to leadership; they are its very essence, guiding leaders through the complexities and challenges of the modern world. Ethical leadership, grounded in unwavering integrity, fosters organizational cultures rich in trust, accountability, and mutual respect, setting the foundation for sustainable success and meaningful impact.

Leaders are thus called upon to not only embrace ethical practices personally but to also cultivate environments that champion these values. It is in the day-to-day decisions, the moments of challenge, and the opportunities for influence that the true nature of ethical leadership is revealed. By embedding ethics and integrity into the fabric of organizational life, leaders can inspire those around them to aspire to higher standards of conduct and to contribute to a collective vision that transcends individual interests.

The journey of ethical leadership is continuous, demanding a commitment to ongoing reflection, learning, and growth. Leaders must remain vigilant, ready to navigate the ethical dilemmas that arise with empathy, fairness, and courage. This commitment to ethical excellence is a potent force for change, capable of transforming organizations and the wider society.

This chapter serves as a call to action for all leaders to embody the principles of ethics and integrity in every aspect of their leadership. By doing so, you pave the way not only for your own success but for the creation of a better, more ethical world. Let the ethical compass of leadership guide you toward decisions that uplift, inspire, and endure, marking your legacy with the indelible imprint of integrity and purpose.

Hypothetical Case Study 1: The Ethical CEO and Environmental Standards

Background: Amidst growing competition and market pressure, the CEO of EcoWear, a sustainable clothing company, faces intense pressure to reduce costs. One proposed solution involves switching to cheaper, non-organic materials that have a significantly higher environmental impact.

Dilemma: The CEO must decide between maintaining the company's commitment to sustainability, which could result in higher costs and potentially reduced market competitiveness, or compromising on environmental standards for short-term financial gains.

Resolution: The CEO decides to uphold the company's stringent environmental and labor standards, focusing on long-term brand integrity and customer trust. To offset the higher costs, EcoWear innovates its production process to become more efficient and invests in community engagement programs that highlight the value of sustainable practices.

Outcome: While initially facing financial strain, EcoWear's commitment to its values strengthens its brand reputation. Over time, the company not only retains its loyal customer base but also attracts new customers drawn by its ethical stance, leading to increased market share and profitability.

Hypothetical Case Study 2: Transparent Leadership During Financial Hardship

Background: During an economic downturn, Alex, a manager at TechSolutions, is faced with the difficult decision of making budget cuts that could lead to layoffs, reduced employee benefits, or decreased project funding.

Dilemma: Alex needs to make decisions that will ensure the company's survival while also considering the welfare and morale of the team. The challenge lies in navigating these financial constraints without compromising on the company's commitment to fairness and employee well-being.

Resolution: Alex opts for transparency, initiating open dialogues with the team to discuss the company's financial situation and potential measures. By involving employees in the decision-making process and considering their input, Alex identifies solutions that distribute the impact more evenly, such as temporary salary reductions for higher-paid staff (including management) to avoid layoffs.

Outcome: This approach not only preserves the team's integrity during a financial crisis but also strengthens the sense of unity and trust within the organization. Employees feel valued and respected, leading to increased loyalty and productivity. As the economic climate improves, TechSolutions emerges stronger, with a committed team ready to drive the company forward.

Key Takeaways: These case studies underscore the importance of adhering to ethical principles and values, even when faced with tough decisions. By prioritizing integrity, transparency, and a commitment to their values, leaders can navigate ethical dilemmas in ways that not only avoid negative outcomes but also positively impact their organization and stakeholders in the long run.

Navigating Ethical Dilemmas Exercise

Objective: This 30-minute exercise is designed to help you think critically about ethical dilemmas in leadership. Instead of applying formal frameworks, you'll use a set of questions to explore these dilemmas and come up with decisions that prioritize integrity.

1. Understand the Dilemma (5 minutes):

Scenario: You are the manager of a small team in a marketing firm. Two of your team members, Alex and Jamie, have both applied for a single promotion to a senior position. Alex has been with the company longer, consistently meets expectations, and is well-liked by the team. Jamie, however, has been with the company for a shorter period but has brought innovative ideas that significantly increased the team's performance and visibility within the company. There's pressure from upper management to promote based on innovation and results to drive the company forward, suggesting Jamie might be the preferred choice. However, promoting Jamie over Alex could demoralize other team members who value loyalty and consistent performance, potentially affecting team harmony and morale. Who would you promote?

2. Analyze Using Critical Questions (10 minutes):

Reflect on and write down your responses to the following questions:

Who gets affected by this decision and how? Consider all stakeholders.

What are the immediate and long-term consequences of possible actions? Think about both positive and negative outcomes.

Does this action align with my personal values and the organization's mission? Reflect on how the decision matches your own ethics and the organization's purpose.

Can I openly discuss my decision with others without hesitation? Gauge the transparency and defensibility of your choice.

3. Group Discussion (15 minutes):

Form a small group and share your thoughts and potential decisions based on your answers.

Together, decide on a course of action that feels ethically sound and justifiable.

4. Conclusion and Share Back (5 minutes):

Briefly, each group shares their chosen course of action and the rationale behind their decision.

Highlight any insights gained or challenges faced in making an ethical decision.

This exercise encourages you to delve into ethical dilemmas using a simple but effective method of questioning. It's designed to prompt critical thinking and ethical consideration without relying on formal frameworks. By questioning the impact of your decisions, aligning them with core values, and considering transparency, you're taking steps toward thoughtful and principled leadership. This approach underscores the importance of ethical decision-making in leading with integrity.

Chapter 3: In-Depth Exploration of ESG Principles

The landscape of global business is witnessing a profound transformation, marked by the ascendancy of Environmental, Social, and Governance (ESG) principles from the peripheries to the core of corporate strategy. This evolution underscores a pivotal shift in how businesses perceive their roles within society and the natural world. ESG principles have emerged as essential elements guiding companies towards sustainable success, aligning business operations with broader societal and environmental objectives.

ESG represents a comprehensive approach that evaluates companies not just on their financial performance but also on how they manage their environmental impact, engage with social concerns, and uphold governance standards. This triad of criteria offers a more holistic view of a company's resilience, ethical stance, and long-term viability. It signals a departure from traditional business metrics, emphasizing that a company's value and values are inextricably linked.

The genesis of ESG as a concept can be traced back to the early 2000s, though its roots are deeper, intertwined with decades of growing environmental awareness, social justice movements, and calls for corporate transparency and accountability. Initially regarded as a niche interest among socially responsible investors, ESG has rapidly gained traction, propelled by mounting evidence that integrating ESG factors into investment decisions can lead to better risk management and superior long-term returns.

Today, ESG stands as a mainstream business imperative, driven by a convergence of factors. Increasingly, consumers demand ethical and sustainable products, employees seek purposeful work with responsible employers, and investors recognize the financial materiality of ESG risks and opportunities. Regulatory bodies worldwide are also beginning to mandate ESG disclosures, further embedding these principles in the corporate fabric.

This chapter delves into the intricate tapestry of ESG, unpacking the significance and application of each pillar — Environmental, Social, and Governance — in the context of contemporary leadership and organizational success. As we explore the evolution, importance, and impact of ESG principles, it becomes clear that they are not just optional add-ons but fundamental components of a strategic framework for businesses aspiring to thrive in today's complex and ever-changing world.

The ESG framework divides into three critical pillars — Environmental, Social, and Governance — each encompassing a range of factors that businesses must navigate to achieve sustainable success. These pillars guide organizations in managing their impact on the world and aligning their operations with ethical, sustainable principles.

Environmental Factors

The environmental pillar focuses on an organization's interaction with the natural world and its stewardship of environmental resources. Key considerations include:

- Climate Change: Addressing carbon emissions and implementing strategies to reduce the organization's climate impact.

- Resource Depletion: Ensuring sustainable use of resources to prevent exhaustion of natural assets.

- Waste Management: Developing efficient systems to reduce, reuse, and recycle waste generated by business operations.

- Biodiversity: Preserving natural habitats and species through responsible business practices.

To mitigate environmental risks and leverage green opportunities, organizations can adopt renewable energy sources, improve energy efficiency, and innovate in sustainable product design. These strategies not only reduce environmental impact but also can lead to cost savings and open up new markets focused on sustainability.

Social Factors

The social pillar examines how a company manages relationships with employees, suppliers, customers, and communities. This includes:

- Labor Practices: Ensuring fair wages, safe working conditions, and respecting workers' rights.

- Community Engagement: Building positive relationships with the communities in which the company operates, often through CSR initiatives.

- Human Rights: Upholding fundamental human rights within the company and the supply chain.

- Diversity and Inclusion: Promoting a diverse workforce and inclusive culture where all employees feel valued and respected.

Businesses can positively impact their workforce and society by fostering a supportive and inclusive work environment, engaging in community development projects, and ensuring their operations and supply chains are free from exploitation. These practices enhance brand reputation, employee satisfaction, and customer loyalty.

Governance Factors

The governance pillar relates to the structures and processes that govern an organization's management and oversight, including:

- Board Composition: Ensuring a diverse and independent board to provide effective oversight.

- Executive Pay: Aligning executive compensation with long-term organizational goals and ethical standards.

- Audits and Internal Controls: Implementing robust financial and operational controls to prevent fraud and mismanagement.

- Shareholder Rights: Respecting the rights of shareholders and ensuring their ability to influence governance.

Effective governance is critical for ensuring accountability, transparency, and ethical business practices. By adhering to high governance standards, organizations can build trust with investors and other stakeholders, mitigate risk, and enhance decision-making.

Through a detailed examination of these ESG factors, organizations can identify areas where they can make meaningful improvements, mitigate risks, and capitalize on opportunities. Embracing the ESG framework not only contributes to a more sustainable and equitable world but also positions companies to thrive in an increasingly complex and interconnected global marketplace.

The journey of Environmental, Social, and Governance (ESG) principles from the margins to the mainstream of business strategy marks a significant shift in the corporate world. This evolution reflects a growing recognition of the interconnectedness of business performance with broader societal and environmental issues. Initially viewed as peripheral concerns, ESG factors have now become central to risk management and value creation, reshaping how companies approach their long-term strategies.

The transformation of ESG into a pivotal element of corporate strategy has been propelled by several key drivers. Regulatory changes around the world have played a crucial role, as governments and international bodies have introduced policies and standards requiring greater transparency and accountability from businesses regarding their environmental and social impacts. This regulatory push has made ESG compliance not just a matter of ethical choice but a legal necessity.

Investor demands have also significantly influenced the ESG agenda. A growing body of evidence suggests that strong ESG practices are linked to better financial performance, lower risks, and enhanced investor returns. As a result, investors are increasingly incorporating ESG criteria into their investment decisions, pushing companies to adopt sustainable practices to attract capital.

Societal expectations have further accelerated the ESG movement. Consumers, employees, and the broader public are demanding more from businesses than just products and services; they expect companies to operate responsibly and contribute positively to society and the environment. This shift in expectations has prompted companies to integrate ESG principles into their operations, branding, and corporate identity.

For contemporary leaders, the rise of ESG represents both a challenge and an opportunity. ESG criteria are reshaping leadership roles and responsibilities, demanding a new set of competencies and a strategic vision that incorporates sustainability and ethical considerations. Leaders are now expected to navigate complex ESG issues, balance diverse stakeholder interests, and make decisions that align with both organizational goals and broader societal values.

Integrating ESG into strategic planning and decision-making processes is crucial. Leaders must ensure that ESG considerations are woven into the fabric of their business strategies, from product development and supply chain management to marketing and customer engagement. This integration enables organizations to identify and mitigate risks associated with environmental and social issues, capitalize on new opportunities for sustainable growth, and build a resilient and ethical business model.

The global impact of ESG on businesses and societies is profound and far-reaching. Companies that embrace ESG principles are not only better positioned to mitigate risks and enhance their competitive advantage but also contribute to the broader goals of sustainable development and social equity. By addressing critical issues such as climate change, resource depletion, inequality, and governance, businesses can play a pivotal role in driving positive change.

The widespread adoption of ESG practices has the potential to catalyze a virtuous cycle, encouraging more businesses to adopt sustainable practices and contributing to a more sustainable and equitable global economy. As ESG continues to gain momentum, its influence on the corporate landscape, leadership roles, and societal progress underscores the importance of sustainability and ethical governance in shaping the future of business and society.

ESG reporting and metrics have become integral components of corporate transparency, accountability, and strategic planning. As organizations worldwide strive to align their operations with Environmental, Social, and Governance (ESG) principles, the need for clear, comprehensive, and standardized reporting has never been more pronounced. This necessity is driven by increasing demands from investors, consumers, regulatory bodies, and other stakeholders for businesses to demonstrate their commitment to sustainable and ethical practices.

The landscape of ESG reporting is characterized by a variety of standards and frameworks designed to guide organizations in measuring and communicating their ESG performance. Among the most prominent are the Global Reporting Initiative (GRI), the Sustainability Accounting Standards Board (SASB), the Task Force on Climate-related Financial Disclosures (TCFD), and the International Integrated Reporting Council (IIRC). Each of these frameworks offers a set of guidelines and metrics tailored to different aspects of ESG reporting, from environmental impact assessments and social responsibility initiatives to governance structures and financial sustainability.

Organizations embarking on the journey of ESG reporting start by identifying the standards and frameworks that align most closely with their operational context, stakeholder expectations, and strategic goals. The choice of framework often depends on factors such as industry sector, geographical location, and the specific ESG issues that are most material to the organization's operations and impact.

Once a reporting framework is selected, organizations proceed to measure their ESG performance against the defined metrics and indicators. This process involves collecting data on a wide range of parameters, such as carbon emissions, water usage, labor practices, diversity and inclusion metrics, and governance structures. The accuracy and integrity of this data collection process are crucial for ensuring the reliability and credibility of the ESG report.

Effective communication of ESG performance is the next critical step. Organizations typically publish annual ESG reports that detail their achievements, challenges, and future commitments in relation to their ESG goals. These reports are designed to be accessible and informative, providing a clear and honest overview of the organization's ESG journey. In addition to traditional reports, many organizations also leverage digital platforms, social media, and interactive tools to engage with stakeholders and share their ESG narratives in dynamic and engaging ways.

The benefits of robust ESG reporting are manifold. It not only enhances transparency and strengthens stakeholder trust but also provides valuable insights that can inform strategic decision-making, risk management, and innovation. By effectively measuring and communicating their ESG performance, organizations can demonstrate their commitment to sustainability and social responsibility, differentiate themselves in the market, and contribute to the broader goals of sustainable development and equitable growth.

ESG reporting and metrics play a pivotal role in operationalizing ESG principles and embedding them into the fabric of organizational life. As the field of ESG continues to evolve, so too will the standards and practices of reporting, underscoring the importance of ongoing engagement, adaptation, and improvement in the pursuit of sustainability and ethical excellence.

As we conclude our exploration of Environmental, Social, and Governance (ESG) principles and their profound impact on the modern business landscape, it becomes unequivocally clear that ESG is not merely a trend but a fundamental shift in how organizations conceive their roles in society and the environment. The critical role of ESG in building sustainable, resilient, and ethical organizations cannot be overstated; it represents a comprehensive framework through which businesses can navigate the complexities of the 21st century, addressing urgent environmental challenges, social inequalities, and the demand for transparent, accountable governance.

The journey through ESG principles has illuminated the multifaceted ways in which these considerations influence every aspect of organizational life, from strategic planning and operational decisions to stakeholder engagement and reporting practices. By integrating ESG criteria, companies not only mitigate risks and enhance their reputations but also unlock opportunities for innovation, growth, and meaningful impact.

At the heart of this transformative journey is leadership. The call to action for leaders at all levels is to embed ESG principles into their leadership ethos and business strategies, recognizing that true leadership excellence is achieved not just through financial success but through contributing positively to the world. Leaders are tasked with the responsibility of steering their organizations toward a future where business success is intrinsically linked with social well-being and environmental stewardship.

To lead with ESG in mind is to embrace a vision of leadership that is forward-thinking, inclusive, and grounded in ethical principles. It requires a commitment to continuous learning, adaptability, and the courage to make decisions that may challenge conventional business paradigms. Leaders must cultivate an organizational culture that values sustainability, champions social responsibility, and practices good governance, setting an example for others to follow.

The imperative for embedding ESG principles into leadership and organizational practices has never been more compelling. As we move forward, let us commit to leading with ESG in mind, recognizing that our decisions today shape the world we live in tomorrow. By aligning our leadership strategies with ESG principles, we pave the way for long-term success that is measured not just in financial terms but in the lasting, positive impact we have on society and the planet. Let this be our collective mission as leaders in the evolving landscape of global business.

Green Tech Innovations Case Study

GreenTech Innovations, a pioneering company in the renewable energy sector, embarked on an ambitious journey to weave Environmental, Social, and Governance (ESG) principles into the fabric of its business model. This strategic pivot was driven by the recognition of sustainability, social responsibility, and robust governance as crucial elements for securing long-term value for all stakeholders, from employees and customers to investors and the communities in which it operated.

The transition to an ESG-focused business model was not without its challenges. GreenTech faced the daunting task of integrating these principles into its core operations, necessitating substantial changes across various domains, including supply chain management, product design, and labor practices. Balancing the diverse interests of stakeholders while maintaining a steadfast commitment to its new ESG-centric approach posed additional complexities, particularly in aligning investor expectations with the company's long-term sustainability goals. Moreover, developing metrics to measure the impact of its ESG initiatives and fostering transparency in its reporting mechanisms required innovative solutions and a dedication to open communication.

Despite these hurdles, GreenTech Innovations discovered significant opportunities in its pursuit of ESG excellence. The company's focus on renewable energy solutions not only tapped into a burgeoning market demand for sustainable products but also established GreenTech as a leader in the green technology sector, distinguishing it from competitors. This strategic positioning, coupled with a robust commitment to ESG principles, attracted socially responsible investors and ESG-focused funds, opening new avenues for funding and growth. Furthermore, the company's clear dedication to environmental and social values resonated deeply with employees and potential hires, particularly those from the millennial and Gen Z demographics, enhancing employee engagement and attracting top talent passionate about making a difference.

The outcomes of GreenTech Innovations' ESG journey were both impactful and inspiring. The company's renewable energy products played a critical role in reducing carbon emissions, aligning with global efforts to combat climate change. Through initiatives focused on fair labor practices and community engagement, GreenTech made significant social contributions, improving lives and fostering community development. Moreover, the company's ESG-centric strategy led to increased market share, higher investor confidence, and sustained growth, demonstrating that ethical business practices and profitability are not mutually exclusive but rather complementary facets of modern business success.

GreenTech Innovations' story exemplifies the nuanced journey of integrating ESG principles into business operations. Through visionary leadership and a unwavering commitment to sustainability, social responsibility, and governance, the company not only navigated initial challenges but also leveraged ESG principles as a catalyst for innovation, growth, and positive impact. This case study stands as a testament to the transformative power of ESG-focused leadership and the potential for businesses to drive meaningful change while achieving long-term success.

Exercise: Integrating ESG Principles into Your Leadership Practice

Objective: This exercise is designed to help you reflect on the importance of Environmental, Social, and Governance (ESG) principles and how they can be integrated into your leadership practices and organizational strategies.

Task Overview: In this exercise, you will analyze a hypothetical scenario related to ESG challenges and opportunities within an organization. You will then develop a strategic plan that embeds ESG principles into the organization's core activities, addressing the identified challenges and leveraging the opportunities for sustainable growth and ethical excellence.

Scenario: Imagine you are a leader at "EcoFriendly Products Inc.," a company specializing in eco-friendly household goods. The company has recently faced criticism for its supply chain practices, which have been linked to environmental damage in sourcing regions and questionable labor practices. On the other hand, there's a growing opportunity to expand into new markets that value sustainability and social responsibility. The company also recognizes the need to enhance its governance to improve transparency and stakeholder engagement.

Instructions:

1. Reflect on ESG Challenges and Opportunities:

- Identify the key ESG challenges and opportunities presented in the scenario.
- Consider the implications of these challenges and opportunities for the company's reputation, operations, and long-term success.

2. Develop an ESG Integration Plan:

- Environmental Strategy: Propose initiatives to minimize the environmental impact of the company's supply chain and product lifecycle. Consider ways to promote sustainability in product design, sourcing, and manufacturing processes.

- Social Strategy: Outline a plan to address labor practices in the supply chain. This might include implementing strict supplier standards, conducting regular audits, and investing in community development projects in sourcing regions.

- Governance Strategy: Suggest improvements in governance to increase transparency and stakeholder engagement. Ideas could include establishing a sustainability committee on the board, enhancing disclosure on ESG performance, and creating channels for stakeholder feedback.

3. Present Your Plan:

Prepare a brief 1-page presentation of your ESG integration plan. Highlight how each element of your plan addresses the identified challenges and leverages opportunities to position "EcoFriendly Products Inc." as a leader in sustainability and social responsibility.

Reflection: After presenting your plan, reflect on the role of leadership in driving ESG integration. Consider the potential impacts of your plan on the organization's culture, stakeholder relationships, and market positioning. Discuss the importance of continuous engagement with ESG principles in adapting to emerging challenges and opportunities in the business landscape.

This exercise not only encourages you to think critically about the application of ESG principles in organizational strategy but also underscores the pivotal role of leadership in navigating the complexities of sustainability, social responsibility, and governance in today's business world.

Chapter 4: The Environmental Dimension: Leading Sustainable Change

In today's world, marked by escalating environmental crises and growing public concern for the planet's health, the imperative for environmental leadership has never been more critical. Leaders across all sectors are called upon to steer their organizations towards practices that safeguard the environment while still achieving business goals. The urgency of addressing environmental challenges cannot be overstated, with climate change, resource scarcity, and pollution posing significant risks to global ecosystems, economies, and communities. However, integrating environmental sustainability into organizational culture and strategy is not merely about mitigating risks; it offers substantial benefits, including innovation, competitive advantage, and alignment with stakeholder values.

At the forefront of the environmental dimension of leadership is the identification of key environmental issues such as climate change, resource scarcity, and pollution. These challenges demand a response from leaders who are informed, committed, and innovative. Climate change, with its vast implications for global weather patterns, sea levels, and biodiversity, requires leaders to adopt long-term, sustainable practices that reduce carbon footprints and enhance resilience. Resource scarcity, another critical issue, challenges leaders to rethink how natural resources are consumed in production processes, pushing for more efficient use and the exploration of renewable alternatives. Pollution, from air and water quality to waste management, calls for strategies that minimize harm and protect public health and the environment.

Leaders can incorporate environmental considerations into their decision-making processes and business models by embedding sustainability into the core values and strategies of their organizations. This involves setting clear environmental goals, measuring and reporting on environmental performance, and integrating sustainability criteria into investment and operational decisions. By doing so, leaders not only contribute to the health of the planet but also build trust with customers, employees, and investors who increasingly demand environmental responsibility from businesses.

Innovative practices for environmental stewardship are vital for moving beyond traditional approaches to sustainability. Leaders can explore and implement cutting-edge technologies and processes that promote energy efficiency, reduce waste, and create sustainable products and services. For instance, adopting circular economy principles can transform waste into resources, creating value through the reuse and recycling of materials. Investing in renewable energy sources not only reduces dependence on fossil fuels but also positions a company as a forward-thinking leader in sustainability.

Engaging stakeholders in environmental initiatives fosters a culture of sustainability throughout the organization and the wider community. Collaborations with governments, NGOs, and other businesses can amplify impact and drive collective action towards environmental goals. Leaders can also champion policies and practices that incentivize sustainable behavior among employees, suppliers, and customers, embedding environmental consciousness into every aspect of organizational life.

The journey towards environmental leadership and sustainable change is both a responsibility and an opportunity for today's leaders. By embracing the environmental dimension of their roles, leaders can guide their organizations towards a future where business success and environmental stewardship are inextricably linked, ensuring a healthier planet for current and future generations.

Building a culture of sustainability within an organization is an essential step for leaders committed to environmental stewardship. This transformative process involves embedding sustainability into the very DNA of the organization, ensuring that every decision, action, and strategy aligns with principles of environmental responsibility. Achieving this cultural shift requires deliberate efforts in communication, education, and engagement, aimed at fostering a collective commitment to sustainability across all levels of the organization.

Communication is the cornerstone of building a culture of sustainability. Leaders must articulate a clear and compelling vision of what sustainability means for the organization and how it relates to the broader mission and values. This vision should be communicated consistently and integrated into all internal and external messaging, from company-wide meetings to marketing materials. By making sustainability a central theme in organizational communication, leaders can ensure that it remains a constant focus and source of inspiration for employees, customers, and other stakeholders.

Education plays a crucial role in empowering employees to contribute to sustainability goals. Leaders should invest in training and development programs that equip employees with the knowledge and skills needed to implement sustainable practices in their work. This could include workshops on energy efficiency, waste reduction techniques, or sustainable sourcing. Additionally, providing resources and tools that enable employees to learn about the environmental impact of their actions fosters a sense of responsibility and agency in contributing to the organization's sustainability efforts.

Engagement is about creating opportunities for employees and other stakeholders to actively participate in sustainability initiatives. This could involve setting up green teams or sustainability committees that give employees a voice in shaping environmental policies and practices. Encouraging employee-led projects, such as community clean-ups or sustainability awareness campaigns, can further enhance engagement and foster a sense of ownership and pride in the organization's environmental achievements. Engaging external stakeholders, including customers, suppliers, and community partners, in sustainability initiatives can also amplify the organization's impact and build strong networks of support for environmental stewardship.

Building a culture of sustainability also requires recognizing and celebrating achievements in this area. Highlighting successes, whether through internal recognition programs or public awards, reinforces the value placed on sustainability and motivates continued effort and innovation. By celebrating these achievements, leaders underscore the positive impact of sustainability on the organization and its stakeholders, further embedding environmental stewardship into the organizational culture.

Fostering a culture of sustainability is an ongoing journey that demands commitment, creativity, and collaboration. Through effective communication, comprehensive education, and meaningful engagement, leaders can cultivate an organizational culture that not only values environmental stewardship but also actively contributes to a more sustainable and resilient future.

Leveraging technology for environmental sustainability represents a dynamic frontier where innovation meets responsibility. Emerging technologies offer unprecedented opportunities to enhance sustainability efforts, from reducing emissions and conserving resources to optimizing processes for greater energy efficiency. As organizations strive to minimize their environmental footprint, the thoughtful selection and integration of these technologies become crucial in aligning operational practices with environmental goals.

Technologies such as renewable energy systems, including solar panels and wind turbines, are at the forefront of reducing dependence on fossil fuels and decreasing greenhouse gas emissions. Similarly, advancements in battery storage technology enhance the viability of renewable energy by addressing the challenge of intermittency and making it possible to store surplus energy for later use.

In operational efficiency, the Internet of Things (IoT) and artificial intelligence (AI) offer transformative potential. IoT devices can monitor and manage energy use in real-time across various operations, identifying areas for improvement and automating energy-saving adjustments. AI and machine learning algorithms can predict energy demand and optimize resource allocation, leading to significant reductions in waste and energy consumption.

Blockchain technology presents another avenue for promoting sustainability through enhanced transparency and traceability in supply chains. By securely recording transactions and tracking the movement of goods, blockchain can verify the sustainability credentials of products and materials, ensuring they meet environmental standards and regulations.

When selecting technology solutions to support sustainability efforts, several considerations come into play. First and foremost, the environmental impact of the technology itself must be assessed, including the resources required for its production, operation, and disposal. The compatibility of the technology with existing systems and processes is also critical to ensure seamless integration and adoption. The selection process should involve a comprehensive analysis of the technology's potential to meet specific environmental goals, considering factors such as scalability, cost-effectiveness, and the ability to provide measurable outcomes. Engaging with stakeholders, including employees, customers, and environmental experts, can provide valuable insights into the suitability and potential impact of different technologies.

Integrating technology solutions for environmental sustainability requires a strategic approach that aligns with the organization's overall sustainability objectives. This may involve pilot projects to test and refine the technology's application, training programs to build internal capacity, and continuous monitoring to assess performance and identify areas for improvement.

Leveraging technology for environmental sustainability offers powerful tools for organizations to reduce their ecological footprint, improve efficiency, and contribute to a more sustainable future. By carefully selecting and integrating technology solutions that align with environmental goals, leaders can drive innovation and sustainability in tandem, setting a course for responsible and resilient business practices in the face of global environmental challenges.

Overcoming the myriad challenges associated with implementing environmental sustainability initiatives demands a nuanced understanding of the obstacles and a strategic approach to navigate through them. Common hurdles include resistance to change within the organization, financial constraints, and the complexity of integrating sustainability into existing business models. Additionally, the evolving nature of environmental regulations and the challenge of measuring the immediate impact of sustainability efforts can further complicate these initiatives.

To surmount these challenges, environmental leaders must exhibit resilience, adaptability, and a commitment to long-term thinking. Resilience is crucial for persevering in the face of setbacks and maintaining momentum towards sustainability goals. Adaptability allows leaders to navigate the changing environmental landscape, adjusting strategies as necessary to remain effective and compliant with new regulations. Long-term thinking is essential for recognizing the ultimate value of sustainability efforts, which may not yield immediate financial returns but are critical for ensuring the organization's sustainability and resilience in the future.

Strategies to overcome obstacles include engaging stakeholders at all levels of the organization to build a shared commitment to sustainability goals. Effective communication that highlights the business case for sustainability can help mitigate resistance to change, demonstrating how environmental initiatives can lead to cost savings, risk reduction, and enhanced brand reputation. Investing in training and development can equip employees with the skills needed to implement sustainable practices, while partnerships with external experts and organizations can provide valuable resources and insights.

Financial challenges can be addressed through strategic planning that identifies cost-effective sustainability initiatives and explores funding options such as grants, incentives, and sustainable investment. Leveraging technology, as previously discussed, can also provide cost-effective solutions for enhancing environmental performance.

As we look to the future, the path forward for environmental leaders is clear. They must play a pivotal role in driving their organizations toward greater environmental sustainability, embedding these principles into every facet of organizational strategy and decision-making. Leaders are encouraged to take bold steps towards sustainability, leveraging the insights and strategies discussed throughout this chapter to effect meaningful change.

This commitment to environmental leadership is not just about mitigating risks or complying with regulations; it's about seizing the opportunity to innovate, to enhance organizational resilience, and to contribute positively to the global community. By championing environmental sustainability, leaders can ensure their organizations not only thrive but also play a crucial role in fostering a sustainable future for all.

The importance of environmental leadership in today's business landscape cannot be overstated. It demands a concerted effort from leaders at all levels to integrate sustainability into the core of their operations and strategies. As we move forward, the vision for the future is one where environmental leadership is not an optional extra but a fundamental aspect of all organizational decision-making and strategy, guiding us towards a more sustainable, equitable, and prosperous world.

Environmental Case Study: EverGreenTech

EverGreenTech, a manufacturing company, embarked on a transformative journey to integrate environmental sustainability into its operations, facing the dual challenges of maintaining productivity and minimizing its environmental impact. The company's comprehensive sustainability program focused on three main areas: achieving zero waste in manufacturing, transitioning to renewable energy, and adopting sustainable sourcing practices. This initiative not only required meticulous planning and investment in long-term solutions but also hinged on engaging employees across all levels and maintaining flexibility to innovate and adapt strategies as needed.

The journey taught EverGreenTech several valuable lessons. First, the importance of setting clear sustainability goals and timelines cannot be overstated, as these serve as benchmarks for tracking progress and maintaining organizational focus on environmental objectives. Secondly, employee engagement emerged as a critical factor in the program's success. By involving employees in the sustainability mission, offering training, and incentivizing innovative ideas, EverGreenTech fostered a culture of innovation and collective commitment to environmental stewardship.

Flexibility and openness to experimentation were also key to overcoming initial challenges. EverGreenTech's willingness to try new approaches and technologies led to significant breakthroughs in reducing waste and emissions. Furthermore, the company learned that collaboration with external partners, including environmental organizations, research institutions, and other businesses, could amplify the impact of its sustainability efforts, sharing knowledge, leveraging new technologies, and advocating for supportive policies.

These insights from EverGreenTech's experience highlight that while specific tactics for implementing sustainability initiatives may vary across different industries and regions, the fundamental principles of planning, engagement, flexibility, and collaboration are broadly applicable. Organizations looking to embark on or enhance their sustainability journey can draw on these principles, adapting them to their unique contexts. This might involve assessing their specific environmental impacts to identify key areas for improvement, cultivating a culture that prioritizes sustainability, exploring innovative technologies and practices, and seeking out partnerships that can expand their impact.

EverGreenTech's story illustrates that with a committed approach to environmental sustainability, organizations can significantly reduce their environmental footprint and emerge as leaders in sustainable practices. The company's journey provides a blueprint for others aiming to navigate the complexities of integrating sustainability into their business models, demonstrating that through commitment, creativity, and collective effort, substantial environmental progress is achievable.

Exercise: Designing Your Sustainability Initiative

In this 30-minute classroom exercise, you're going to dive into the process of identifying an environmental challenge within your organization and creating a plan for a sustainability initiative tailored to address it. You'll learn to set clear goals, outline a plan, kickstart the initiative, and think about how to measure its success.

Let's Get Started:

Step 1: Identify Environmental Challenges (5 minutes)

Start by jotting down a few environmental issues your organization might be facing. These could range from high water usage to inefficient recycling systems, or even broader challenges like the environmental impact of your supply chain.

Step 2: Choose Your Challenge (5 minutes)

From your list, pick one challenge that stands out as either particularly pressing or where you see a great opportunity for positive change. This will be the focus of your sustainability initiative.

Step 3: Setting Your Goals (5 minutes)

For the challenge you've selected, set some SMART goals. An example could be, "Implement a comprehensive recycling program that reduces waste by 30% in one year."

Step 4: Planning Your Initiative (5 minutes)

Outline a basic action plan for achieving your goals. Think about the steps needed, such as researching recycling options, engaging stakeholders for support, and determining the resources you'll need. Also, consider any obstacles you might encounter and how you could overcome them.

Step 5: Implementing the Plan (5 minutes)

Detail the immediate steps to launch your initiative. Who needs to be involved? What's the timeline? Assign specific tasks and deadlines. For example, the first step could be to form a "green team" by the end of the month.

Step 6: Measuring Success (5 minutes)

Reflect on how you will evaluate the impact of your sustainability initiative. Will you look at waste reduction metrics, participant feedback, or perhaps energy savings? Decide on how you'll track progress and measure outcomes.

Sharing and Feedback:

If there's time, pair up with a classmate to discuss your plans. Share insights, offer feedback, and think about how you might support each other's initiatives. This is a great opportunity to refine your approach and consider new perspectives.

This exercise is designed to empower you as an emerging leader to tackle environmental challenges head-on. By planning and implementing a sustainability initiative, you're taking an important step towards making a tangible difference. Remember, effective sustainability efforts start with clear goals, strategic planning, and a commitment to measuring and celebrating progress.

Chapter 5: Social Responsibility: Cultivating Inclusivity and Well-being

In the evolving landscape of modern leadership, social responsibility stands out as a defining factor, shaping how organizations interact with their employees, local communities, and broader societal systems. This chapter delves into the critical role of social responsibility within the context of purpose-driven leadership. It explores why integrating social responsibility into organizational culture and strategy is not only an ethical imperative but also a strategic necessity that enhances trust, strengthens brand reputation, and supports long-term success.

Social responsibility extends beyond mere philanthropy or compliance; it involves a profound commitment to creating positive impacts through ethical business practices. This commitment is increasingly recognized as essential for attracting talent, driving innovation, and building resilience against social risks. At the core of social responsibility are principles such as ethical labor practices, community engagement, and the protection of human rights, which define how a business operates within its social environment. Ethical labor practices ensure that employees are treated with fairness and respect, fostering a loyal and motivated workforce. Community engagement acts as a bridge between businesses and the societies they operate in, enhancing the social license to operate. Upholding human rights within corporate strategies reflects a commitment to global standards that transcend local legal requirements, positioning businesses as leaders in global citizenship.

The profound impact of social responsibility on various stakeholders is undeniable. Employees seek meaningful work environments that respect their rights and provide opportunities for growth, while communities benefit from corporate engagement that supports local development. Societies at large thrive when businesses contribute positively to setting higher social standards.

Creating a workplace culture that values diversity, equity, and inclusion (DEI) is integral to social responsibility. Developing strategies that promote such a culture involves implementing DEI training, establishing transparent hiring practices, and supporting policies that promote inclusivity at every level of the organization. The benefits of an inclusive culture are extensive, leading to greater creativity, better problem-solving, higher employee satisfaction, and ultimately, improved organizational performance.

Leaders also play a crucial role in advocating for and implementing policies that support employee well-being and work-life balance. Comprehensive health programs, flexible working arrangements, and mental health support not only contribute to employee well-being but also enhance overall productivity and organizational loyalty. Engaging with communities is another essential aspect of social responsibility. This involves listening to community needs, engaging in long-term projects, and measuring the impact of these initiatives. Effective community engagement can develop partnerships that are mutually beneficial, enhancing the organization's social license to operate.

Implementing social responsibility initiatives can present challenges, including resource allocation, measuring impact, and aligning initiatives with business objectives. Yet, these challenges also present opportunities for innovation and leadership in social responsibility. Leaders who successfully navigate these challenges can drive significant change and position their organizations as leaders in corporate responsibility. Leaders are encouraged to take proactive steps toward enhancing their organization's social responsibility efforts, fostering inclusive, well-being-oriented cultures, and using their influence to drive positive social impacts. The vision for the future is one where leadership is synonymous with active social responsibility, where business success is measured not just by financial outcomes but by the positive changes made in people's lives and communities.

Social responsibility in leadership goes beyond mere corporate obligation; it is an integral component of purpose-driven leadership, where the ultimate goal transcends profit to include making a meaningful impact on society. Within this context, social responsibility is defined by the deliberate actions a leader takes to positively influence the social systems in which their organization operates. This may encompass a range of activities—from ensuring fair labor practices and promoting employee well-being to engaging with communities and safeguarding human rights.

The importance of social responsibility in building trust with stakeholders cannot be overstated. When leaders demonstrate a commitment to ethical practices and societal contributions, they not only enhance their organization's reputation but also foster deeper trust and loyalty among customers, employees, and investors. This trust is essential for sustained success, as it solidifies the company's standing in the market and shields it against the reputational damage that can arise from unethical practices.

A strong reputation for social responsibility can significantly enhance an organization's attractiveness, making it a preferred choice for top talent and conscientious consumers. In the long term, this reputation contributes to financial stability and growth, as more consumers and job seekers opt for companies with strong ethical standards. The essence of social responsibility in the corporate sector is encapsulated in its three key components: ethical labor practices, community engagement, and human rights protection.

This includes providing fair wages, ensuring safe working conditions, and fostering respectful and dignified treatment of all employees. It also involves creating opportunities for professional development, which helps in nurturing a motivated and skilled workforce. Effective community engagement involves understanding and acting on the needs of the local communities where an organization operates. This could mean investing in local infrastructure, supporting educational programs, or sponsoring local events. Such engagement not only improves the community's quality of life but also builds a positive image of the company, strengthening its social license to operate. Upholding human rights within corporate strategies is crucial. This means ensuring that the company's operations do not contribute to human rights abuses and that they actively promote human rights wherever possible. For example, a company might implement stringent controls to prevent forced labor in its supply chain or use its influence to advocate for human rights policies in challenging environments.

The impact of these social responsibility initiatives is profound. Employees who work for socially responsible companies often report higher job satisfaction and a greater sense of purpose. Communities that benefit from corporate social responsibility efforts can experience enhanced economic development and improved living conditions, which contribute to social stability and growth. On a broader scale, the commitment of businesses to social responsibility helps advance societal progress, pushing the envelope on what it means to be a responsible business in today's world.

The role of social responsibility in leadership is pivotal—it reshapes how leaders and their organizations are viewed by the world and how they impact the society they are part of. By integrating social responsibility into their core strategies, leaders not only drive their organizations towards greater economic success but also towards a more sustainable and equitable future.

Building inclusive cultures within organizations is a strategic imperative that goes beyond mere compliance to embody a core value system centered around diversity, equity, and inclusion (DEI). Leaders play a critical role in fostering these cultures by implementing strategies that not only acknowledge diversity but also actively support and celebrate it. This includes creating policies that promote equity in hiring, salary, and promotion processes, and cultivating an environment where diverse perspectives are respected and valued.

The benefits of such an inclusive culture are manifold. Organizations that embrace DEI tend to experience increased innovation, as a variety of perspectives lead to more creative solutions and ideas. Employee satisfaction also improves when individuals feel respected and valued for their unique contributions. This, in turn, enhances decision-making processes, as decisions are made from a wider range of viewpoints and experiences, leading to outcomes that better reflect the needs and desires of a diverse workforce and client base.

In addition to fostering inclusivity, modern leaders must also prioritize social well-being, advocating for and implementing policies that support employee well-being and work-life balance. This aspect of social responsibility involves understanding and addressing the needs of employees, ensuring they have access to resources that support both their professional and personal development. Whether through flexible working arrangements, comprehensive health benefits, or support services, initiatives that promote well-being help in building a workforce that is not only more productive but also happier and more committed to the organization.

Such efforts in promoting social well-being and building inclusive cultures are not just beneficial internally; they also enhance the organization's reputation externally. They make the company attractive not only to potential employees but also to customers and partners who are increasingly looking to engage with socially responsible organizations. In the grand scheme, these practices contribute to a cycle of positivity that enhances corporate performance and impacts the broader society positively.

By integrating these values into their leadership ethos, leaders not only ensure the long-term success of their organizations but also contribute to the creation of a more just and equitable society.

Engaging with communities is a pivotal aspect of an organization's social responsibility efforts. This engagement represents a commitment to the broader societal fabric in which a company operates, reinforcing its role as a responsible stakeholder. Effective community engagement not only helps address specific local needs but also builds enduring relationships that can support long-term business success.

The best practices for meaningful community involvement typically start with listening. By understanding community needs directly from the source, organizations can tailor their initiatives to have the most impact. Partnering with local leaders and organizations already embedded within the community can also enhance the effectiveness and reach of engagement efforts. These partnerships can provide valuable insights into the community's culture and dynamics, which helps in designing programs that are respectful and appropriate. Furthermore, consistent involvement rather than one-off projects tends to have a deeper impact, establishing trust and demonstrating genuine commitment to the community's welfare.

Transparency about goals and outcomes is another best practice that underpins successful community engagement. Sharing what the organization aims to achieve and reporting back on results can help maintain open communication channels and build trust. This transparency, coupled with a willingness to adjust initiatives based on community feedback, demonstrates adaptability and genuine interest in the welfare of the community, rather than just ticking a box for corporate social responsibility.

Implementing these social responsibility initiatives is not without challenges. Leaders often face hurdles such as aligning business objectives with social goals, managing resource allocation, and measuring the impact of their initiatives. Additionally, there can be skepticism from both within the organization and from external stakeholders about the motives behind social responsibility efforts.

To overcome these challenges, leaders need to integrate social responsibility into the core business strategy, making it an integral part of how the company operates rather than a side project. Training and involving employees at all levels can also foster an organizational culture that values and practices social responsibility. Moreover, using data-driven approaches to measure the impact of community engagement initiatives can provide clear evidence of their value, helping to secure ongoing support from internal and external stakeholders.

The opportunities for leaders to drive change through committed social responsibility practices are significant. By addressing these challenges head-on, leaders can enhance their organization's reputation, foster employee pride and satisfaction, and build stronger community ties. In the long term, these efforts can lead to greater business resilience and success, as companies that are seen as beneficial to their communities tend to attract more loyalty from customers, better engagement from employees, and more favorable conditions from local governments. The significance of community engagement within social responsibility cannot be overstated. By adopting best practices and embracing the challenges and opportunities it presents, leaders can make a substantial positive impact on their communities and society at large, paving the way for a future where businesses and communities thrive together.

As we conclude this exploration of social responsibility within the framework of purpose-driven leadership, it is clear that the role of social responsibility extends far beyond the boundaries of traditional business practices. It is integral to creating organizational cultures that are not only inclusive and oriented toward well-being but also robust and resilient in the face of changing societal expectations.

Throughout this discussion, we have seen how social responsibility enriches leadership, enhances corporate reputations, and fosters trust among stakeholders. It also plays a crucial role in attracting and retaining talent, as more individuals seek employment with companies that reflect their values and are committed to making a positive impact on the world.

Leaders are therefore encouraged to take proactive steps to enhance their social responsibility efforts. This involves not only embedding social responsibility into the core strategies and operations of their organizations but also continually assessing and adapting these strategies to meet new challenges and opportunities. By doing so, leaders not only drive their organizations toward greater success but also contribute to the well-being of their employees, the communities they interact with, and society at large.

Looking ahead, the vision for the future of leadership is one where social responsibility is not an optional add-on but a fundamental aspect of every decision and action. In this future, leaders leverage their influence to promote inclusivity, well-being, and positive social impacts, creating an environment where businesses thrive by contributing to the prosperity of society. This is a future where the success of an organization is measured not just by its financial performance but by the depth and breadth of its positive impact on the world. Leading with social responsibility is more than a leadership style—it is a commitment to a sustainable and equitable future. It is a call to action for all leaders to rise and shape a world where business practices and societal well-being are inextricably linked, ensuring that the legacy they leave is as enduring as it is benevolent.

Case Example: Horizon Enterprises

Consider the case of Horizon Enterprises, a technology firm that has successfully integrated various initiatives to enhance social well-being, demonstrating a comprehensive approach to social responsibility. This company recognized early on that the well-being of its employees directly influences productivity, creativity, and overall job satisfaction, which are crucial for long-term success.

Health and Wellness Programs

Horizon Enterprises launched a "Total Well-being" program that focuses on both physical and mental health. The program includes free gym memberships, weekly yoga classes held in the office, and a monthly session with a wellness coach who provides personalized guidance to employees on managing stress and achieving work-life balance. To address mental health, Horizon also introduced confidential counseling services, which employees can access remotely, ensuring privacy and convenience. These initiatives have led to a noticeable decrease in reported stress levels and a significant improvement in employee morale.

Flexible Work Arrangements

Understanding the diverse needs of its workforce, Horizon implemented flexible work arrangements to promote a better work-life balance. Employees can choose from various options such as telecommuting, flexible hours, and a compressed workweek which allows employees to work four longer days and take the fifth day off. This flexibility has been particularly beneficial for working parents and employees pursuing further education, enabling them to better manage their personal commitments alongside their professional responsibilities.

Community Service Activities

Horizon Enterprises has also embedded social responsibility into its corporate identity by actively engaging in community service activities. The company established a volunteer program that partners with local nonprofits focused on education and environmental conservation. Each quarter, employees are encouraged to spend a day volunteering, fully paid, at a choice of partner organizations. Horizon also matches employee donations to these charities, doubling the financial support provided to these causes. These activities not only aid the community but also foster a sense of teamwork and pride among employees.

Impact and Recognition

The initiatives at Horizon Enterprises have not only enhanced employee satisfaction and retention but have also attracted media attention and industry accolades for corporate responsibility. Employee feedback has been overwhelmingly positive, with many citing the supportive work environment as a key factor in their decision to stay with the company long-term. Community partners have praised Horizon for its contributions, further enhancing the company's reputation in the marketplace.

Horizon Enterprises' comprehensive approach to social well-being through health programs, flexible work arrangements, and community involvement serves as an exemplary model for other organizations aiming to enhance their social responsibility efforts. These initiatives illustrate how integrating social well-being into corporate strategy can yield substantial benefits for both the organization and the wider community, establishing a strong foundation for sustainable success.

Exercise: Developing a Diversity and Inclusion Plan

This exercise is designed to guide you through the process of assessing your current organizational culture and developing a comprehensive plan to enhance diversity, equity, and inclusion (DEI) within your organization. By the end of this activity, you should have a clear set of objectives, actionable steps, and methods for measuring progress in building a more inclusive workplace.

Step 1: Assess Current Culture

Survey: Distribute anonymous surveys to employees to gather candid feedback on their perceptions of the organization's inclusivity. Questions should cover areas such as perceived fairness, opportunities for advancement, and comfort in voicing diverse opinions.

Focus Groups: Conduct focus group discussions with employees from various backgrounds to dive deeper into issues that might not be fully captured in the survey.

Review Policies and Practices: Examine existing HR policies and practices for recruitment, promotion, and compensation to identify any potential biases or barriers that could affect diversity and inclusion.

Step 2: Identify Areas for Improvement

Data Analysis: Compile and analyze the data collected from surveys, focus groups, and policy reviews to identify patterns and areas needing attention.

Priority Setting: Based on the analysis, determine which areas are most critical and set priorities for addressing them. These might include improving hiring practices, enhancing support for underrepresented groups, or increasing leadership diversity.

Step 3: Set Objectives

Specific Goals: Establish clear, measurable goals for each priority area. For example, increase the representation of underrepresented groups in leadership roles by 20% within three years.

Broad Objectives: Set broader objectives that focus on cultural change, such as achieving a certain score on employee satisfaction surveys regarding inclusivity.

Step 4: Develop Action Plans

Actionable Steps: For each objective, outline specific actions to be taken. This could include initiatives like bias training, establishing mentorship programs for underrepresented employees, or creating a diversity task force.

Timeline: Assign a timeline for each action, specifying deadlines and milestones to ensure progress is made and maintained.

Step 5: Implement the Plan

Launch Initiatives: Begin rolling out the initiatives as planned. Ensure that all employees are informed of the changes and understand the importance of these efforts for the organization's success.

Communication: Maintain open lines of communication throughout the implementation phase. Keep employees updated on progress and developments related to the DEI initiatives.

Step 6: Measure Progress

Regular Check-Ins: Schedule regular check-ins to evaluate the progress against the set objectives. This could be done through follow-up surveys, additional focus groups, or performance reviews of DEI initiatives.

Adjustments: Be prepared to make adjustments to the plan based on feedback and the results from these check-ins. DEI is an ongoing process that may require fine-tuning as initiatives are implemented and new challenges emerge.

Step 7: Review and Refine

Annual Reviews: Conduct an annual review of the overall diversity and inclusion plan to assess its effectiveness and make necessary adjustments.

Continuous Improvement: Foster a culture of continuous improvement by encouraging feedback and suggestions from all employees on how to enhance DEI efforts.

By following these steps, you can create a robust diversity and inclusion plan that not only addresses immediate areas for improvement but also sets the foundation for a continually evolving culture that values and embraces diversity. This structured approach ensures that DEI initiatives are strategic, systematic, and capable of making significant impacts on your organization's culture and effectiveness.

Chapter 6: Governance for the Future: Ethical Structures and Accountability

Governance stands as a critical pillar in the foundation of any organization, crucial for establishing and maintaining ethical leadership and organizational integrity. In this chapter, we delve into why robust governance practices are not merely administrative necessities but essential frameworks that sustain ethical operations and foster trust among stakeholders. The relationship between strong governance, trust, and long-term organizational success is deeply intertwined. Effective governance structures ensure that an organization operates transparently and accountably, which in turn solidifies stakeholder trust and secures the organization's reputation and operational longevity.

At its core, governance involves the systems, processes, and policies through which an organization is controlled and directed. It is about aligning the interests of all stakeholders, including shareholders, management, customers, suppliers, financiers, the government, and the community. However, governance extends beyond compliance and oversight; it is a broader embodiment of the organization's commitment to ethical principles and integrity in all aspects of its operations.

The role of governance structures is crucial in supporting ethical decision-making and leadership practices. These structures—which include the board of directors, audits, compliance programs, and ethical guidelines—serve as the backbone for enforcing standards and practices that uphold the organization's values. They provide a framework within which decisions are made, ensuring that these decisions are transparent and align with both legal requirements and ethical standards.

Effective governance structures facilitate accountability by clearly delineating responsibilities and establishing rigorous oversight mechanisms. This accountability ensures that decision-makers at all levels are answerable for their actions and the outcomes of those actions. Furthermore, governance frameworks support ethical leadership by providing guidelines and resources that help leaders navigate complex ethical dilemmas. These structures also foster a culture of integrity that permeates the entire organization, influencing everything from strategic planning to day-to-day operations.

In the context of organizational ethics and integrity, governance also involves proactive engagement with the ethical dimensions of business. This includes regular reviews of governance practices to address emerging ethical challenges and adapt to changing regulatory landscapes. It also involves engagement with stakeholders to understand their expectations and concerns regarding ethical conduct and governance.

We will explore detailed examples and strategies that demonstrate how governance can be effectively leveraged to support ethical leadership and enhance organizational integrity. Through a discussion of best practices, case studies, and theoretical insights, we aim to provide a comprehensive understanding of how governance serves as the bedrock of ethical leadership and long-term success in any organization. By embedding strong governance principles, leaders can ensure their organizations are not only compliant but also champions of ethical business practices, ready to face the challenges of the modern business environment with resilience and integrity.

Enhancing transparency in leadership is fundamental to cultivating trust and accountability within any organization. Transparency ensures that stakeholders, including employees, investors, customers, and the broader community, can see and understand the actions and decisions of leaders. This openness is crucial not only for maintaining credibility but also for fostering a culture of trust that can significantly enhance organizational resilience and performance.

Leaders can improve transparency in several ways. Firstly, in operations, leaders should strive to make business processes visible and understandable to all stakeholders. This might involve open forums or regular updates where operational strategies and results are discussed openly. In decision-making, transparency can be achieved by involving various stakeholders in the decision-making process through consultative councils or feedback mechanisms that allow for a broader range of input and visibility into the processes that lead to decisions.

When it comes to reporting, leaders should ensure that all organizational reports—financial, environmental, social—are comprehensive, understandable, and accessible. These reports should not only adhere to high standards of accuracy and integrity but should also be disseminated widely to ensure that all stakeholders have an opportunity to review and assess the organization's performance and strategies. Enhanced reporting transparency can include detailed disclosures about the company's governance practices, ethical standards, and risk management strategies.

In parallel, fostering accountability in organizations is an essential counterpart to enhancing transparency. Accountability in leadership refers to the obligation of the organization's leaders to account for their activities, accept responsibility for them, and disclose the results in a transparent manner. Ensuring accountability involves setting up mechanisms such as performance reviews, audits, and compliance checks that help maintain high standards of ethical behavior and decision-making.

These mechanisms should be clearly outlined and implemented across all levels of the organization, from the top executives to entry-level employees. This could involve regular training sessions on the organization's ethical standards, the establishment of clear policies regarding conduct and governance, and the creation of accessible channels for reporting unethical behavior without fear of retribution.

The role of accountability in reinforcing ethical behavior cannot be overstated. It not only ensures that ethical breaches are dealt with promptly and effectively but also promotes a culture where such behavior is the exception rather than the norm. Accountability frameworks help to align the actions of individuals with the organization's values and objectives, promoting a consistent approach to ethical decision-making.

Enhancing transparency and fostering accountability are critical components of effective leadership. They ensure that leaders not only act ethically but are also seen to act ethically, thus building stakeholder trust and contributing to the long-term success of the organization. As we explore these concepts further, it becomes clear that both transparency and accountability are indispensable in nurturing a robust and ethical organizational culture.

Implementing effective governance structures is crucial for ensuring that an organization upholds ethical leadership and maintains integrity across all its operations. These structures are designed to facilitate clear decision-making processes, enforce accountability, and ensure compliance with laws and regulations. Best practices for designing and implementing these governance structures focus on creating systems that not only monitor and control but also empower and innovate within the organization.

One key practice in establishing effective governance structures involves clearly defining roles and responsibilities. This clarity helps prevent overlaps and gaps in authority and accountability. Each role within the organization, from the board of directors to frontline employees, should have well-defined duties and a clear understanding of how these duties contribute to the broader organizational goals.

Another best practice is the establishment of robust oversight mechanisms. These include regular audits, both internal and external, and other checks such as risk assessments and compliance reviews. These mechanisms ensure that the organization adheres to ethical standards and legal requirements, providing early detection of potential issues before they escalate.

Transparency mechanisms are also vital. This involves creating clear channels through which information about organizational practices and decisions is communicated to relevant stakeholders. Transparency not only reinforces accountability but also builds trust with employees, investors, customers, and the public.

Incorporating diverse perspectives in governance structures is increasingly recognized as a best practice. Diversity on boards and in leadership positions can enhance decision-making processes by bringing a wider range of experiences and viewpoints. This diversity helps in considering the interests of all stakeholders and in fostering innovative solutions to complex problems.

While strong governance controls are essential for ensuring accountability and compliance, they must be balanced with the need for organizational agility. Too rigid a governance structure can stifle innovation and slow decision-making, which can be detrimental in a rapidly changing business environment. To achieve this balance, organizations can adopt a tiered approach to governance, where decision-making authority is delegated based on the level of risk involved. Routine decisions that carry minimal risk can be handled at lower levels of the organization to ensure responsiveness and flexibility. In contrast, decisions that are more complex and carry significant risks or ethical implications should involve higher levels of scrutiny and broader consultations.

Flexible governance frameworks can also adapt to changing conditions. This involves regularly reviewing and updating governance policies and structures to reflect new challenges and opportunities. Such flexibility allows the organization to remain dynamic and forward-looking while still maintaining strong governance principles.

Regular training and development programs for everyone in the organization, especially those in leadership and governance roles, ensure that all individuals understand their roles within these structures and are equipped to perform them effectively. Continuous education on emerging trends, legal changes, and best practices in governance keeps the organization at the forefront of ethical leadership.

Implementing effective governance structures is a critical aspect of maintaining organizational integrity and ethical leadership. By adhering to best practices in governance and finding the right balance between control and agility, organizations can protect themselves against risks while remaining adaptable and innovative. This dual focus not only enhances compliance and ethical standards but also positions the organization for long-term success and trustworthiness in the eyes of all stakeholders.

The board of directors plays a pivotal role in governance, serving as the cornerstone of oversight and ethical leadership within any organization. Their responsibilities extend beyond fiduciary duties to include setting the tone at the top, shaping corporate policies, and ensuring that the organization's strategic objectives align with its ethical standards and long-term goals. As such, the effectiveness of the board directly influences the organization's ability to uphold its commitments to stakeholders and maintain high standards of integrity and accountability.

To enhance the effectiveness of boards and ensure their alignment with organizational values and goals, several strategies can be implemented. Firstly, ensuring diversity within board composition is crucial. A diverse board brings a variety of perspectives, experiences, and skills, which can enrich decision-making processes and enable the board to better address complex organizational challenges. Diversity also promotes a more comprehensive understanding of the customer base, workforce, and global market trends, which are essential for effective governance. Another key strategy is the continuous education of board members on the latest developments in the business environment, regulatory changes, and emerging risks. This ongoing training helps board members stay informed about factors that might impact the organization and ensures they are prepared to respond effectively. Additionally, it's beneficial to conduct regular performance evaluations of the board. These assessments can help identify areas where the board is performing well and areas where improvements are needed, ensuring that the board continues to function effectively and adapts to new challenges.

Setting clear expectations and defining the roles and responsibilities of board members can significantly enhance board effectiveness. This clarity helps prevent overlaps and conflicts within the board and ensures that each member knows what is expected of them in terms of oversight and contribution to strategic discussions.

The board should also actively engage in succession planning to ensure that leadership transitions are smooth and do not disrupt the organization's governance or strategic direction. Effective succession planning involves identifying future leaders whose values and vision align with those of the organization and preparing them through mentorship and leadership development programs.

In fostering a culture of transparency, the board must ensure that its actions and decisions are communicated clearly to all stakeholders. This openness not only reinforces the board's accountability but also builds trust both within the organization and with external stakeholders. The role of boards in governance is critical not just for compliance and oversight but also for instilling a culture of ethical leadership. By implementing strategies that enhance board effectiveness and ensure alignment with the organization's values and goals, boards can lead by example, steering their organizations toward sustainable success and ethical integrity.

Overcoming challenges in governance is essential for maintaining the integrity and effectiveness of any organization. Common challenges often include maintaining independence on the board, managing conflicts of interest, and ensuring effective communication between the board and other stakeholders. Addressing these challenges requires targeted strategies that not only resolve current issues but also strengthen the governance framework to prevent future problems.

One significant challenge is ensuring the independence of board members. Independence is crucial for unbiased decision-making and effective oversight. Organizations can address this by instituting policies that limit the number of insider directors and define clear criteria for what constitutes independence. Regularly rotating board assignments and committee memberships can also help to maintain a fresh perspective and prevent entrenchment.

Conflicts of interest present another persistent challenge. These can undermine trust and lead to decisions that do not align with the best interests of the organization or its stakeholders. To manage conflicts of interest, it is vital to establish a robust process for their disclosure. Organizations should require board members to disclose any potential conflicts regularly and recuse themselves from related discussions and decisions. Creating a culture where such transparency is valued and encouraged is key.

Effective communication between the board, management, and other stakeholders is essential for coherent governance. Misalignments and misunderstandings can lead to poor decision-making and strategies that are not aligned with the organization's goals. Enhancing communication can involve regular and structured reporting systems, open sessions with stakeholders, and the use of collaborative technologies that keep all parties informed and engaged.

The importance of continuous governance improvement cannot be overstated. As the business environment evolves, so too must governance practices. This means regularly reviewing and updating governance structures and policies to reflect new risks, regulatory changes, and best practices. Continuous improvement might involve periodic training sessions for board members on the latest governance trends and challenges, as well as the adoption of new technologies that enhance governance processes.

Adopting a proactive approach to governance improvement helps organizations to not only address current challenges but also to anticipate and mitigate future risks. This ongoing commitment to strengthening governance structures ensures that an organization remains resilient, adaptable, and aligned with the best interests of all stakeholders. This approach not only upholds the integrity of governance practices but also enhances the overall sustainability and success of the organization.

Governance serves as a fundamental pathway to ethical leadership, providing the structural backbone necessary for building and sustaining organizations committed to integrity and ethical standards. This chapter has underscored the pivotal role of governance in ensuring that organizations not only comply with laws and regulations but also exceed them in pursuit of higher ethical objectives. Governance frameworks instill a culture of accountability, transparency, and fairness, which are indispensable for any organization aiming to operate ethically and sustainably. Leaders must recognize the critical importance of robust governance structures and prioritize them within their strategic plans. Effective governance does not merely prevent ethical breaches and ensure compliance; it actively promotes a positive organizational culture by setting a tone of integrity that permeates all levels of the organization. Leaders who embrace governance as a cornerstone of ethical leadership help forge organizations that are resilient and trusted by their stakeholders.

This call to action for leaders is to integrate governance deeply and irreversibly into the fabric of organizational life. By doing so, leaders not only safeguard the interests of their stakeholders but also set their organizations on a course of long-term success. The commitment to strong governance structures should be viewed as a continuous journey, involving regular assessment, adaptation, and improvement to meet evolving challenges and opportunities.

Looking forward, we can envision a future where governance, transparency, and accountability are not just regulatory requirements but fundamental aspects of every organization's ethos and operation. In this future, governance is the norm, not the exception, characterized by leaders who not only preach ethical values but also practice them through transparent and accountable governance practices. Such a future promises organizations that are not only more ethical but also more successful and more resilient in the face of the complex challenges of the modern world. Leaders of today and tomorrow have the opportunity—and the responsibility—to forge this future. By prioritizing governance and embedding it in the DNA of their organizational culture, leaders can ensure that ethical leadership is more than just an ideal; it becomes the defining characteristic of their organizational success.

Salesforce: A Model of Innovative Governance

Salesforce, founded in 1999, quickly rose to prominence not just for its revolutionary CRM solutions but also for its commitment to social responsibility and corporate governance. The company's leadership, under CEO Marc Benioff, has consistently prioritized governance as a key component of its corporate strategy. Salesforce's governance framework is built on the principles of transparency, accountability, and stakeholder engagement. One of the core elements of its governance strategy is the establishment of an independent board of directors, which includes experts from various fields who provide diverse perspectives on company operations and strategic decisions. This independence ensures that the board can perform its oversight role without undue influence from management.

Salesforce has implemented a comprehensive Code of Conduct that outlines the ethical responsibilities of all employees and executives. The company enhances this code with regular training sessions and an open-door policy that encourages employees to report any ethical concerns without fear of retaliation. Additionally, Salesforce has established a robust compliance program that monitors and enforces adherence to both internal policies and external regulatory requirements. The company is also noted for its stakeholder engagement practices. The company regularly conducts stakeholder panels and surveys to gather feedback on its governance practices and corporate strategies. This feedback is crucial for ensuring that the company's governance remains aligned with stakeholder expectations and evolving industry standards.

Governance at Salesforce extends into its approach to sustainability and social responsibility. The company has set ambitious targets for renewable energy use and carbon neutrality, with clear reporting and accountability mechanisms to track progress. Moreover, Salesforce's 1-1-1 model, where it contributes one percent of its technology, people, and resources to support nonprofit organizations, demonstrates how governance frameworks can be leveraged to achieve social impact.

Salesforce's governance and ethical leadership have earned it numerous accolades, including regular rankings as one of the world's most ethical companies by the Ethisphere Institute, and top placements in lists of best places to work. These honors reflect the company's success in integrating robust governance practices with high business performance.

The governance practices at Salesforce have not only contributed to its substantial business success but have also enhanced its reputation among customers, investors, and employees. The company's commitment to ethical governance has built a strong foundation of trust and loyalty, which in turn drives its continued growth and innovation. Salesforce exemplifies how effective governance can transcend basic compliance to become a driver of corporate success and ethical business leadership. The company's ongoing commitment to governance innovation serves as a powerful model for other organizations striving to enhance their own governance practices and ethical standards.

Exercise: Evaluating Governance Practices

This exercise is designed to help leaders assess and enhance their organization's current governance structures and practices. Through a structured review process, leaders will identify strengths, weaknesses, and areas for improvement, fostering a governance system that supports ethical practices, accountability, and organizational integrity.

Objective: To conduct a comprehensive evaluation of your organization's governance structures and practices to identify areas of strength and opportunities for improvement.

Materials Needed:

- Governance assessment template
- Organizational governance documents (e.g., bylaws, codes of conduct, board of directors' structure)
- Feedback forms for participants

Step 1: Gather Existing Governance Documents

Collect all relevant documents that outline your organization's governance practices, including bylaws, codes of conduct, policies on board structure and functions, and any recent audit or compliance reports.

Step 2: Develop an Assessment Template

Create an assessment template that will guide the evaluation process. This template should include key governance areas such as:

- Board structure and independence
- Ethical guidelines and compliance mechanisms
- Stakeholder engagement practices
- Transparency and reporting procedures
- Conflict of interest policies

Step 3: Review and Rate Current Practices

Using the assessment template, review each governance area. Rate each area on a scale (e.g., 1-5, where 1 is poor and 5 is excellent) based on how well current practices meet industry standards and organizational goals. Consider involving a cross-functional team for this evaluation to ensure diverse perspectives.

Step 4: Identify Strengths and Weaknesses

Analyze the ratings and comments from the review. Identify areas where your organization excels and where it falls short. Strengths might include robust conflict of interest policies or effective board oversight, while weaknesses could be gaps in stakeholder engagement or lack of transparency in decision-making processes.

Step 5: Solicit Feedback

Distribute feedback forms to a broader range of stakeholders, including board members, senior executives, and other employees. Ask for their insights on the effectiveness of current governance practices and suggestions for improvement. This step ensures that the evaluation considers multiple viewpoints and is as comprehensive as possible.

Step 6: Compile Findings and Plan for Improvement

Compile the findings from the review and feedback. Create a detailed report that summarizes the strengths, weaknesses, and suggested improvements. Develop a strategic action plan that outlines specific steps to enhance governance practices. This plan should include:

- Clear objectives for each area of improvement
- Assigned responsibilities to ensure accountability
- Timelines for when changes should be implemented
- Metrics for measuring the effectiveness of new practices

Step 7: Review and Update Regularly

Governance is not a set-it-and-forget-it component of an organization. Schedule regular reviews (e.g., annually) of governance practices to ensure they remain effective and aligned with organizational goals and external regulations. Adjust the governance structures and practices as necessary to meet evolving challenges and opportunities.

This exercise is a critical step towards strengthening governance within your organization. By systematically evaluating governance practices and implementing targeted improvements, you can ensure that your organization upholds the highest standards of integrity and accountability. This not only enhances internal operations but also reinforces trust among stakeholders, positioning your organization for long-term success.

Chapter 7: Resilience in Leadership: Navigating Challenges with Purpose

In today's complex, fast-paced, and unpredictable global landscape, the capacity for resilience has become a crucial attribute for leaders across all sectors. The challenges confronting today's organizations range from rapid technological changes and economic fluctuations to environmental crises and social transformations. Such a landscape demands leaders who are not only skilled and knowledgeable but also profoundly resilient. Resilience in leadership involves more than merely surviving; it's about thriving amidst adversity and navigating challenges with foresight and grace.

Resilience, especially in the context of purpose-driven leadership, is fundamentally about the ability to maintain a steadfast pursuit of one's organizational and personal goals despite setbacks, pressures, or unexpected changes in the environment. It involves a dynamic combination of personal integrity, emotional intelligence, and an unwavering commitment to one's core values and vision. This quality enables leaders to steer their organizations through crises and uncertainties, ensuring that they emerge not only intact but strengthened and more aligned with their core mission.

The significance of resilience in leadership cannot be overstated. It is this trait that often distinguishes successful organizations from those that falter under pressure. Resilient leaders are able to view challenges as opportunities for growth and learning, adapting their strategies to meet new demands without losing sight of their long-term goals and values. Such leaders are adept at managing stress, both their own and that of their teams, and can turn adversity into a catalyst for team cohesion and innovation.

We now dive into the nature of resilience, exploring how it can be cultivated and strengthened within leaders and their teams. We will examine the strategies that resilient leaders employ to overcome challenges, and the role that purpose-driven leadership plays in enhancing organizational resilience. By understanding and embodying the principles of resilience, leaders can ensure that their organizations not only withstand the trials of the modern world but also excel, driving forward with clarity and vigor.

Resilience in leadership is underpinned by several key attributes that enable leaders to navigate the complexities of the modern business environment effectively. These pillars of resilience—adaptability, perseverance, emotional intelligence, along with a clear purpose and strong values—are essential for leaders who aspire to guide their organizations through times of uncertainty and change.

Adaptability is perhaps one of the most crucial attributes of resilient leadership. It refers to the ability of leaders to adjust their strategies, expectations, and tactics in response to changing circumstances without veering off course from their ultimate goals. Adaptability requires an open mind and a willingness to embrace change, even when it deviates from the original plan. This flexibility allows leaders to respond to new opportunities and challenges in a way that can propel their organization forward rather than holding it back.

Perseverance is the steadfastness leaders need to demonstrate in the face of difficulties. It is about maintaining a commitment to achieving organizational goals despite obstacles, setbacks, or failures. Perseverance is fueled by a deep-seated determination and a tenacious work ethic. It involves the resilience to recover from setbacks with renewed energy and to continue pursuing objectives with a clear focus, recognizing that the path to success is often paved with challenges that require patience and sustained effort.

Emotional intelligence plays a pivotal role in leadership resilience by enabling leaders to manage their own emotions and those of others effectively. Leaders with high emotional intelligence are adept at recognizing and regulating their feelings and using this awareness to make informed, empathetic decisions. They are also better equipped to support their teams through stressful times, foster a positive work environment, and navigate interpersonal dynamics smoothly, all of which are vital during periods of uncertainty.

Alongside these traits, a clear purpose and strong values are foundational to fostering resilience. Knowing the 'why' behind their actions provides leaders with a guiding light that remains constant, even when the business landscape is in flux. This sense of purpose, combined with firmly held values, offers a framework for making decisions that are not only strategic but also ethical. Leaders who are clear about their purpose and values are less likely to be swayed by adversity. Instead, they use their core beliefs as a compass to steer their organizations through challenges, making choices that align with long-term objectives and the overall mission of the organization.

Together, these pillars form the backbone of resilience in leadership, equipping leaders with the tools and mindsets necessary to overcome obstacles and lead their organizations to success. In the following sections, we will explore strategies to cultivate these qualities, ensuring leaders are prepared to face the demands of their roles with strength, adaptability, and a clear vision for the future.

Building personal resilience is essential for leaders to effectively manage the diverse challenges of modern leadership roles. This section explores practical techniques for developing personal resilience, including stress management, mindfulness, and maintaining a growth mindset. It also highlights the importance of self-care and setting boundaries to sustain long-term leadership effectiveness.

Effective stress management is crucial for maintaining mental and emotional resilience. Leaders can adopt various stress-reduction techniques such as regular physical exercise, deep breathing exercises, and structured relaxation methods like meditation or yoga. Additionally, time management strategies, such as prioritizing tasks and delegating responsibilities, can significantly reduce stress levels by preventing work overload and promoting a more manageable workload.

Mindfulness involves being fully present and engaged in the current moment without judgment. For leaders, practicing mindfulness can enhance focus, reduce stress responses, and improve decision-making capabilities. Techniques to foster mindfulness include meditation, mindful walking, or simply taking intentional breaks throughout the day to refocus and reconnect with one's environment and inner state. Regular practice helps leaders remain centered and calm, even in high-pressure situations.

A growth mindset, as defined by psychologist Carol Dweck, is the belief that abilities and intelligence can be developed through dedication and hard work. Leaders with a growth mindset see challenges as opportunities to learn and grow, rather than as insurmountable obstacles. To cultivate this mindset, leaders should embrace challenges, persist in the face of setbacks, learn from criticism, and find lessons in the success of others. This approach not only builds resilience but also encourages a culture of continuous improvement within the organization.

For sustained resilience and effectiveness, leaders must also prioritize self-care and set clear boundaries. This means recognizing one's limits and not consistently working beyond capacity. Leaders should ensure they get adequate rest, engage in hobbies or activities that rejuvenate their spirit, and spend time with loved ones. Setting boundaries might involve defining work hours, managing accessibility, and learning to say no when necessary to maintain a healthy work-life balance.

Building personal resilience is also supported by having strong personal and professional support systems. This includes relationships with peers, mentors, and family who provide emotional support and practical advice. Leaders should cultivate these relationships and seek regular feedback to gain new perspectives and sustain their resilience.

Developing personal resilience requires intentional practice and commitment to self-improvement and self-care. By adopting these techniques, leaders not only enhance their own capacity to handle stress and adversity but also set a powerful example for their teams, thereby fostering a resilient organizational culture. The techniques outlined above equip leaders with the tools needed to navigate the complexities of their roles effectively and sustainably.

Cultivating organizational resilience is a strategic endeavor that requires embedding resilience into the culture, policies, and practices of an organization. This process ensures that resilience becomes a core characteristic of the organization, enabling it to respond dynamically to challenges and opportunities alike. Here, we explore strategies for building this essential quality into the organizational framework and discuss how to create an environment that fosters risk-taking, learning from failure, and continuous improvement.

The foundation of organizational resilience lies in its culture. Cultivating a resilient culture involves promoting values and norms that support adaptability, flexibility, and a collective commitment to overcoming challenges. Leaders play a crucial role in this by modeling resilient behaviors, such as showing composure under pressure, being open to change, and demonstrating perseverance. Additionally, recognizing and rewarding resilience in employees encourages those behaviors, reinforcing a culture where resilience is valued and emulated.

Organizational policies and practices should support the resilience of its workforce. This includes implementing flexible work arrangements that allow employees to balance personal and professional demands effectively. Policies should also encourage employees to take initiative and make decisions, which fosters a sense of autonomy and empowerment. Furthermore, establishing clear communication channels ensures that employees at all levels are informed about organizational issues and changes, which is critical in times of crisis or uncertainty.

A resilient organization is one that not only tolerates risk but actively encourages it within a framework that manages potential downsides. Creating an environment that supports risk-taking involves defining clear risk boundaries within which employees can operate. Leaders should encourage experimentation and innovation, emphasizing that calculated risks can lead to valuable learning and growth. By removing the stigma associated with failure and instead celebrating the lessons learned from these experiences, organizations can foster a more innovative and resilient workforce.

One of the hallmarks of a resilient organization is its ability to learn from failure. To facilitate this, organizations should implement processes for analyzing failures and extracting valuable insights without assigning blame. Conducting post-mortem reviews on projects or initiatives that didn't achieve the desired outcomes can help identify both weaknesses in execution and potential areas for improvement. Sharing these learnings across the organization enhances collective knowledge and prevents future missteps.

Continuous improvement is integral to organizational resilience. It involves regularly reviewing and refining processes, products, and services in response to new information and feedback. Establishing continuous improvement mechanisms, such as quality circles, suggestion boxes, and regular review meetings, helps ensure that the organization remains responsive and adaptive to changes in its internal and external environments. Cultivating organizational resilience is a comprehensive approach that integrates resilience into every aspect of the organization's culture, policies, and practices. By encouraging risk-taking, learning from failures, and committing to continuous improvement, leaders can build organizations that are not only equipped to handle today's challenges but are also prepared to capitalize on future opportunities. This proactive stance on resilience positions organizations to thrive in an increasingly complex and unpredictable business landscape.

Navigating challenges with purpose requires leaders to leverage their organization's core purpose and values as a compass during times of crisis or uncertainty. This approach ensures that decisions and actions remain aligned with what the organization fundamentally stands for, providing stability and direction when it is most needed.

In times of crisis, the clarity of purpose and strong values serve as critical anchors, helping leaders and their teams to focus on what truly matters. These core principles become the basis for all strategic decisions, ensuring that even under pressure, the organization does not veer off course. For instance, a company that values customer trust above all else will prioritize transparency and honesty in its communications during a product recall, thereby strengthening relationships despite the setback.

Using purpose and values as guiding principles also involves communicating these core elements effectively to all stakeholders. During uncertain times, employees, customers, investors, and other stakeholders look to leaders for reassurance and direction. Clear communication about how the organization's purpose and values are guiding its responses can build confidence and foster a collective sense of commitment and resilience.

Aligning actions with organizational values during a crisis can often require innovative approaches. Leaders might need to adapt strategies quickly while ensuring that these adaptations do not compromise the organization's values. For example, a business might shift to remote work to continue operations during a health crisis while also ramping up its IT support to maintain its commitment to employee support and productivity.

Leveraging purpose and values during challenging times also means making tough decisions that can test the organization's commitments. Leaders may face scenarios where short-term sacrifices are necessary to uphold long-term values. Decisions that might seem difficult in the immediate term can ultimately reinforce the organization's integrity and the trust placed in it by its stakeholders. Navigating challenges is not just about staying true to the organization's identity; it's also about using that identity as a strategic asset to steer through crises and uncertainties. By consistently applying their core principles, leaders not only provide steady guidance during turbulent times but also strengthen their organization's resilience and trustworthiness, positioning it for recovery and future success.

The importance of building and nurturing supportive networks is paramount, particularly for enhancing resilience in leadership and within organizational contexts. These networks provide critical support, guidance, and encouragement, enabling leaders to navigate challenges more effectively and fostering a collaborative spirit that can elevate the entire organization.

Supportive networks, both within and outside the organization, offer a range of benefits. They serve as sounding boards for new ideas, sources of emotional support during tough times, and pools of diverse expertise and perspectives that can help solve complex problems. These relationships can fortify a leader's ability to withstand stress and recover from setbacks more quickly.

For leaders looking to cultivate such networks, several approaches can be effective. Prioritizing genuine connections is crucial; focus on building relationships based on mutual respect and genuine interest rather than merely forming connections for potential future gain. Authentic relationships are more likely to provide meaningful support and are stronger and more reliable in times of need. Leaders should also be proactive in their networking efforts. This can involve actively seeking out opportunities to meet new people and strengthen existing relationships through industry conferences, participation in professional associations, and engagement in community events. Regular interaction keeps relationships vibrant and ensures your network is there when you need it.

Offering help generously is another key to building supportive networks. Regularly offering help—not just reaching out when you need something—establishes you as a valuable and supportive network member. This might mean sharing resources, providing mentorship, or offering insightful advice.

In today's digital world, leveraging technology can help in maintaining and expanding networks. Utilize professional social media platforms, such as LinkedIn, to connect with peers worldwide. Online forums, professional groups, and virtual conferences can also be excellent resources for expanding your network.

Encouraging a supportive culture within your organization can also be beneficial. Leaders can facilitate networking by organizing team-building activities and cross-departmental projects that help employees form connections across the organization. Building networks that include people from different industries, backgrounds, and experiences can provide broader insights and innovative ideas. Diversity within your network ensures a wider range of support and a richer array of perspectives, enhancing creative problem-solving and decision-making. Maintaining regular communication with your network through updates, check-ins, and shared insights helps keep relationships strong and ensures that your connections are informed about your challenges and successes. By nurturing a supportive network, leaders not only enhance their own resilience but also contribute to a more supportive, interconnected, and robust organizational culture. These networks become invaluable assets in times of crisis, providing the external support necessary to complement internal resources and capabilities.

Leading through change with resilience is a crucial skill for leaders, particularly in times of organizational transformation. Effective change leadership not only drives the organization forward but also ensures that teams remain motivated and focused on the mission. This involves a blend of clear communication, transparency, and inclusivity—key elements that foster a supportive environment conducive to successful change management.

When leading organizational change, the first step is to articulate a clear vision of what the change is and why it is necessary. This vision provides a sense of direction and purpose, helping team members understand not only the practical aspects of the change but also how it aligns with the organization's broader goals. Leaders must communicate this vision effectively and repeatedly, ensuring that it resonates across all levels of the organization.

Transparency is another critical component of leading through change. It involves openly sharing the progress of the change efforts, including both successes and setbacks. By being transparent about the challenges and how they are being addressed, leaders can build trust and credibility. This openness not only helps in managing expectations but also allows team members to feel genuinely involved in the process, which can be crucial for maintaining morale and motivation.

Inclusivity in change management means involving employees in the change process. This can be achieved by seeking their input and feedback through meetings, surveys, or focus groups. When team members are included in planning and decision-making, they are more likely to buy into the change, feel valued, and commit to the organization's new direction. Furthermore, inclusivity helps harness diverse perspectives, which can lead to more innovative and effective solutions to the challenges that arise during the change process. In addition to these strategies, resilience in change leadership also requires an emphasis on supporting and developing the workforce. This includes providing training and resources that employees need to adapt to new roles or systems. It also involves acknowledging and addressing the emotional impact of change. Leaders should create opportunities for team members to express their concerns and questions. Responding empathetically to these concerns and providing clear, supportive responses can alleviate anxiety and build a stronger team cohesion.

Celebrating milestones and recognizing contributions throughout the change process can significantly enhance team motivation. Acknowledging both individual and team achievements helps reinforce the value of the work being done, boosting morale and encouraging continued effort toward the change objectives.

As we conclude our exploration of resilience in leadership, it is evident that resilience is not just a desirable trait but a fundamental necessity for purpose-driven leaders and organizations aiming to navigate the complex challenges of the future. This chapter has underscored the importance of resilience, emphasizing how it empowers leaders and their teams to withstand adversity, adapt to change, and emerge stronger.

Resilience equips leaders with the tools to maintain focus on their mission despite uncertainties and setbacks. It enables organizations to transform challenges into stepping stones for innovation and growth. Therefore, it is crucial for leaders to continually develop their resilience capabilities. This ongoing development involves enhancing personal resilience through self-care, stress management, and emotional intelligence, as well as cultivating organizational resilience by building strong teams, maintaining flexible strategies, and fostering an inclusive and supportive culture.

Leaders are encouraged to view challenges not merely as obstacles but as opportunities for learning and growth. This perspective shift can redefine an organization's approach to problem-solving and innovation, encouraging a more proactive and positive engagement with the inevitable changes of the business landscape. By adopting this mindset, leaders can instill a sense of purpose and optimism within their teams, even in the face of difficulties. They have a critical role in modeling resilience for their organizations. By demonstrating adaptability, perseverance, and a steadfast commitment to ethical principles and organizational goals, leaders can inspire others within their organizations to embrace these qualities. The ability to model resilience effectively communicates that these are not just values to aspire to but are practical and essential qualities for success.

The call to action for leaders, therefore, is to embody and champion resilience in all aspects of organizational life. By doing so, leaders not only navigate their organizations through the currents of change but also chart a course toward a more robust and dynamic future. As resilience becomes embedded in the fabric of organizational culture, it shapes a workforce that is not only equipped to handle the demands of the present but is also prepared and excited for the opportunities of the future.

Case Study: Satya Nadella's Transformation of Microsoft

When Satya Nadella took over as CEO of Microsoft in 2014, the company was perceived as lagging behind its competitors in key areas such as cloud computing, mobile technology, and innovation culture. Microsoft was known for its aggressive and often isolating corporate environment, which was increasingly seen as out of step with the evolving tech industry.

Nadella faced the dual challenge of revamping Microsoft's product offerings while simultaneously transforming its corporate culture. The tech landscape had shifted dramatically, with cloud computing and mobile devices becoming dominant. Microsoft needed to pivot swiftly to avoid falling further behind. Moreover, Nadella recognized that Microsoft's culture of internal competition was hindering its ability to innovate and adapt.

Nadella's leadership was distinctly purpose-driven, guided by the principle of "empathy," which he believed was crucial not only to personal life but also to the design of technology and business strategy. His vision for Microsoft centered on the core values of respect, integrity, and accountability. Nadella steered Microsoft to focus on building technology that empowers people and organizations around the world to achieve more.

Cultural Transformation: Nadella encouraged a shift from a "know-it-all" to a "learn-it-all" culture, emphasizing personal growth, collaboration, and openness over individual success and competition. This shift was critical in fostering an environment where innovative ideas could be nurtured and executed.

- Focusing on Synergy and Integration: Recognizing the disjointed operations within the company, Nadella pushed for greater synergy and integration among different departments. This approach helped streamline operations and leveraged Microsoft's diverse product suite as a comprehensive platform rather than isolated offerings.

- Investing in Technology and Innovation: Under Nadella's leadership, Microsoft invested heavily in cloud computing and AI technology. The launch of Azure as a robust cloud service competitor to Amazon Web Services marked a significant turnaround in Microsoft's business strategy.

- Acquisitions and Partnerships: Nadella oversaw strategic acquisitions like LinkedIn and GitHub, integrating them into Microsoft's ecosystem to enhance the company's capabilities in social media and open-source software, respectively.

Nadella's focus on culture and purpose-driven leadership led to a remarkable turnaround for Microsoft. The company regained its position as a tech leader, with significant growth in cloud computing and new technologies. Employee morale soared as the new culture took root, fostering innovation and attracting top talent. Financially, Microsoft's market capitalization reached new heights, making it one of the most valuable companies in the world.

Satya Nadella's leadership of Microsoft demonstrates how purpose-driven leaders can successfully navigate complex challenges by staying true to their core values. By transforming Microsoft's corporate culture and aligning the company's operations with its mission to empower every person and every organization on the planet to achieve more, Nadella not only revitalized its product offerings but also reinvigorated its global influence. This case study exemplifies the profound impact that empathetic and value-driven leadership can have on a global scale, confirming that the core values of respect, integrity, and accountability are indeed compatible with and even essential to business success.

Exercise: Crafting a Resilience Plan

This guided exercise is designed to help you assess your current level of resilience and identify specific areas for development, both personally and within your organization. By following these step-by-step instructions, you will create a personalized resilience plan that enhances your ability to handle stress, adapt to change, and recover from challenges effectively.

Step 1: Assess Your Current Resilience

Self-Assessment: Begin by reflecting on recent challenges you've faced, both personally and professionally. How did you respond to these challenges? What were the outcomes? Use a simple scale from 1 to 10 (where 1 is not resilient and 10 is highly resilient) to rate your response to each situation.

Feedback Collection: Ask for feedback from colleagues, friends, or family about your resilience. This could be in the form of specific examples when they observed resilient behaviors in you or times when they think you could have handled a situation better.

Step 2: Identify Areas for Development

Analysis: Review the self-assessment and feedback to identify patterns. Are there particular types of situations where your resilience is lower? Are there common skills or responses that you could improve (e.g., maintaining positivity, stress management, problem-solving)?

Goal Setting: Based on your analysis, set specific, measurable, achievable, relevant, and time-bound (SMART) goals to enhance your resilience. For example, if stress management is an area for improvement, a goal could be, "Practice mindfulness meditation for 10 minutes each day for the next 30 days."

Step 3: Create Your Personal Resilience Plan

Action Steps: For each goal, outline detailed action steps. If your goal is to practice mindfulness meditation, an action step could be to enroll in a mindfulness course or download a meditation app.

Resources Identification: Determine what resources you will need to achieve your goals. This might include books, courses, apps, or support from a mentor or coach.

Timeline: Establish a timeline for each action step. This will help keep you accountable and track your progress.

Step 4: Develop Organizational Resilience Strategies

Team Assessment: Conduct similar resilience assessments with your team or department. Identify common areas where resilience could be strengthened.

Plan Development: Collaborate with your team to develop strategies that enhance organizational resilience. These might include team-building activities, resilience training, or creating a more supportive workplace culture.

Implementation Schedule: Set timelines and assign responsibilities for implementing resilience strategies within your organization.

Step 5: Review and Adjust

Regular Review: Schedule regular check-ins (e.g., monthly or quarterly) to review your personal resilience plan and the organizational strategies. Assess progress, celebrate achievements, and make adjustments as necessary.

Continuous Learning: Encourage ongoing learning and adaptation by seeking new resources, participating in workshops, and staying informed about best practices in resilience development.

By completing this exercise, you'll not only have a clearer understanding of your current resilience levels but also a practical plan for enhancing your ability to navigate life's challenges. This proactive approach will empower you and potentially your team to thrive in an ever-changing world, reinforcing both personal growth and organizational success.

Chapter 8: Mapping Your Impact: Understanding and Applying Materiality

In the realm of Environmental, Social, and Governance (ESG) initiatives, the concept of materiality plays a pivotal role in defining the focus and scope of an organization's efforts. Materiality helps organizations determine which aspects of ESG are most significant to their business operations and stakeholder groups. This prioritization is crucial not only for effective resource allocation but also for enhancing the impact and relevance of the organization's sustainability initiatives.

Understanding and applying materiality within an ESG framework involves identifying and responding to economic, environmental, and social issues that substantively affect the organization's ability to create, preserve, or erode economic value, as well as environmental and social value for itself and its stakeholders. For purpose-driven leadership, this understanding guides decision-making and strategy development, ensuring that efforts are not dispersed across too broad an array but are concentrated where they can achieve the greatest benefit.

Materiality serves as a strategic tool for leaders by directing their attention and resources toward the most pressing ESG issues relevant to their specific organizational context. This focus is informed by a thorough analysis of the organization's operations, industry standards, and stakeholder expectations. By aligning ESG initiatives with what is material to the organization, leaders can ensure that their actions not only comply with regulatory requirements but also resonate more deeply with investors, customers, and employees, thereby enhancing stakeholder engagement and trust.

The relationship between materiality, stakeholder expectations, and organizational values and goals is intricate. Stakeholders today, whether they are investors, employees, customers, or community members, expect organizations to operate responsibly and transparently, particularly regarding issues that significantly impact their lives and the environment. These expectations shape perceptions of the company and influence its reputation and financial performance. As such, materiality assessments need to be dynamic and responsive to evolving stakeholder concerns and environmental conditions.

By integrating stakeholder feedback into the materiality assessment process, organizations can gain valuable insights into which issues are perceived as most critical by those directly affected by the company's operations. This stakeholder-informed approach not only helps in prioritizing ESG efforts but also aligns these efforts with the organization's broader values and long-term goals. For example, if a technology company identifies data privacy as a material issue for its stakeholders, focusing on enhancing data security measures and transparent reporting can reinforce its commitment to protecting user information, thereby supporting its core value of trust.

The application of materiality in ESG initiatives enables organizations to report more effectively on their sustainability performance. By concentrating on material aspects, companies can provide more meaningful and useful information in their sustainability reports, which stakeholders can use to make informed decisions. This targeted reporting demonstrates an organization's commitment to accountability and its ability to respond to the most significant impacts of its operations.

Understanding and applying materiality within the ESG framework is essential for purpose-driven leaders aiming to create sustainable and impactful organizational practices. It ensures that their initiatives are not only strategically aligned with the organization's objectives and values but also finely tuned to stakeholder needs and expectations. Through this focused approach, leaders can effectively contribute to sustainable development while enhancing their organization's competitive edge and reputation in the marketplace.

In the context of Environmental, Social, and Governance (ESG) reporting and strategy, materiality refers to the process of identifying and prioritizing the ESG issues that are most likely to impact an organization's business performance and its stakeholders' decisions significantly. It determines which topics are important enough to be reported on and addressed through corporate strategies, based on their potential influence on both the organization and its broader ecosystem of stakeholders, including investors, customers, employees, and the community.

Key Aspects of Materiality in ESG:

- Financial Impact: Materiality assesses whether an ESG issue is likely to affect the financial condition or operating performance of the company. This includes understanding how these issues might influence revenue, profitability, or capital expenditure. For example, how might climate change regulations impact the cost structure of a manufacturing firm?

- Stakeholder Influence: Materiality involves considering the interests and concerns of stakeholders who are affected by the organization's activities or whose actions can affect the company's ability to execute its strategy. This requires engagement with stakeholders to gather insights into their views and priorities concerning ESG issues.

- Risk Management: Identifying material ESG factors is crucial for effective risk management. It helps companies anticipate and mitigate potential risks that could threaten their business model or reputation. For instance, a business might consider labor practices and supply chain management as material if poor practices could pose significant regulatory or reputational risks.

- Strategic Alignment: Materiality in ESG also ensures that the focus on certain issues aligns with the organization's broader strategic goals, values, and vision. It ensures that the company is not just reacting to external pressures but is proactively managing those ESG aspects that align with its long-term objectives.

- Dynamic and Context-Specific: The determination of what is material is dynamic and specific to each organization's context, including industry, geography, and operational scope. What is considered material for a tech company in Silicon Valley might be different from what is material for a mining company in South Africa.

Understanding and implementing a materiality assessment is crucial for aligning organizational strategy with material Environmental, Social, and Governance (ESG) factors. A variety of tools and frameworks have been developed to aid organizations in identifying and prioritizing these issues effectively.

Several methodologies are available to conduct a materiality assessment, each offering unique insights and structured approaches. The Global Reporting Initiative (GRI) provides a comprehensive framework widely used for this purpose, helping organizations identify, gather, and report information on impacts that are significant to their business and stakeholders. The Sustainability Accounting Standards Board (SASB) offers industry-specific standards that help pinpoint which ESG issues are likely to impact financial performance, guiding strategic focus. Additionally, the International Integrated Reporting Council (IIRC) promotes an integrated approach to materiality, considering all relevant factors that affect an organization's ability to create value over time. Many organizations also employ a materiality matrix, a visual tool that maps the significance of various issues against the level of stakeholder concern and the potential impact on the business, aiding in the prioritization of key issues.

These tools help align the organization's strategy with material ESG factors by identifying key issues, assessing their impact and relevance, and integrating ESG into decision-making. For example, SASB standards can guide strategic focus by highlighting relevant ESG issues, while frameworks like GRI can evaluate how each ESG issue affects operations and stakeholders, ensuring that strategy addresses the most significant impacts. Through integrated reporting, companies can factor ESG considerations into their broader business strategy, ensuring sustainable value creation.

The process begins with preparation, defining the scope and objectives of the assessment and deciding which frameworks and tools will be used based on industry relevance and stakeholder needs. Stakeholder identification follows, listing all relevant groups such as investors, employees, customers, and community groups, and determining the method and level of engagement for each group. Data is then collected using surveys, interviews, focus groups, industry reports, sustainability indices, and peer benchmarks. Analysis and prioritization apply the chosen framework to analyze the collected data, using tools like the materiality matrix to visualize and prioritize issues based on their significance and stakeholder concern. The findings are then reviewed with senior management and key stakeholders for validation and integrated into the organization's strategic planning and reporting processes. Regularly revisiting the materiality assessment is essential to reflect changes in the business environment, stakeholder expectations, and organizational strategy.

To ensure a comprehensive understanding of material issues, it's important to actively involve stakeholders throughout the assessment process. This involves keeping stakeholders informed about the goals and processes of the materiality assessment through transparent communication. Inclusive engagement uses diverse methods such as surveys and workshops to collect insights from all stakeholder groups, and feedback integration incorporates stakeholder feedback into the final assessment to ensure their concerns and insights are adequately reflected.

By following these guidelines and employing the appropriate tools and frameworks, organizations can conduct effective materiality assessments that enhance their ability to manage ESG issues strategically and responsively. This approach not only aligns with best practices in sustainability but also bolsters the organization's resilience and capacity for long-term value creation.

When dealing with Environmental, Social, and Governance (ESG) aspects, identifying material issues is just the first step. Prioritizing these issues based on their impact on the organization and its stakeholders is crucial for effective management and integration into business strategies. This process ensures that resources are allocated efficiently and that the organization's actions resonate most strongly with stakeholder expectations and business objectives.

The prioritization of material issues often involves assessing the potential impact of each issue on the organization's financial performance, reputation, and operational effectiveness. It also considers the concerns and values of stakeholders, ensuring that the issues that matter most to them are given appropriate attention in the organization's strategy, operations, and reporting.

Once material issues have been prioritized, integrating them into the business strategy involves several key steps. First, it's essential to ensure that the leadership team understands the importance of these issues and is committed to addressing them. This may involve training sessions, workshops, and regular discussions to embed these issues into the leadership's strategic thinking.

Operational integration is the next step, where material issues are embedded into daily business processes. This could involve adjusting procurement policies to ensure sustainable sourcing, modifying production processes to reduce environmental impact, or implementing new HR policies that enhance diversity and inclusion. Each operational change should align with the prioritized material issues and contribute to the organization's overall ESG objectives.

Reporting on material issues is also critical. Stakeholders, including investors, customers, and regulatory bodies, expect transparent communication about how an organization is addressing its most significant ESG issues. Effective reporting should not only detail the actions taken and the outcomes achieved but also explain how these actions align with the organization's broader strategic goals. This transparency helps to build trust and can enhance the organization's reputation.

Integrating materiality into business strategy and operations can sometimes be challenging, primarily if it necessitates significant changes in established processes or involves considerable investment. Leaders must manage these challenges by maintaining clear communication with all stakeholders about the benefits of addressing material issues—not just for the company but for society at large.

The integration of materiality requires continuous assessment. As market conditions, regulatory environments, and stakeholder expectations evolve, so too must the organization's approach to managing material issues. Regularly revisiting and reassessing the organization's materiality assessment ensures that the strategy remains relevant and effective. Prioritizing and integrating material issues into an organization's strategy, operations, and reporting is a dynamic and ongoing process. It requires commitment from all levels of the organization and a clear understanding of how these issues align with the organization's long-term goals and values. By effectively managing material issues, an organization can not only mitigate risks but also capitalize on opportunities that enhance long-term sustainability and success.

The concept of materiality is pivotal in guiding organizations through the complexities of today's business landscape, where Environmental, Social, and Governance (ESG) concerns significantly influence corporate success. Materiality helps organizations identify and focus on issues that are not only crucial to their operational and financial performance but also essential to their stakeholders, ranging from investors and employees to communities and regulators.

Understanding and prioritizing material issues is more than a compliance or reporting requirement; it is a strategic imperative that drives meaningful change and sustainable success. By focusing on what truly matters, organizations can allocate resources more effectively, enhance their reputational strength, and achieve greater operational efficiencies, all of which contribute to long-term sustainability.

Leaders are encouraged to continuously engage with the concept of materiality, recognizing its dynamic nature. As external conditions and stakeholder expectations evolve, so too must the organization's approach to identifying and managing material issues. This ongoing engagement requires a proactive stance, where materiality assessments are regularly updated and recalibrated to reflect current realities and future forecasts. Furthermore, leaders should view materiality not just as a tool for risk management but as a strategic framework that can guide their organization's journey towards sustainable excellence. Effective use of materiality assessments allows leaders to map their impact accurately, identifying areas where their organization can make significant positive contributions to society and areas where there is potential for improvement.

As a call to action, leaders across all sectors are urged to leverage materiality assessments as a core part of their strategic planning and decision-making processes. By doing so, they can ensure that their strategies are robust, their impacts are positive, and their practices align with the highest standards of social, environmental, and corporate governance. This commitment to understanding and prioritizing material issues will not only propel organizations towards their goals but also elevate their role as stewards of sustainability in the modern world. Materiality is a powerful lens through which leaders can view and shape their strategies, ensuring that their actions resonate deeply with their values and aspirations for the future. As businesses continue to navigate the challenges and opportunities of the 21st century, those that embrace and effectively manage their material issues will be best positioned to thrive in an increasingly complex and demanding global market.

Case Study: Materiality in Action at Unilever

Unilever, a global leader in consumer goods, has long been recognized for its robust approach to sustainability and its effective use of materiality assessments to enhance its Environmental, Social, and Governance (ESG) impact. The company's Sustainable Living Plan, launched in 2010, set ambitious targets to decouple its growth from environmental impact while increasing its positive social impact.

Unilever's approach to materiality involves a continuous process of engaging with stakeholders to identify and prioritize issues that are crucial both for the business and for society. The company conducts regular materiality assessments that combine extensive stakeholder consultations with a deep analysis of business trends and societal expectations. These assessments help Unilever focus its efforts on the most impactful areas, such as sustainable sourcing, waste reduction, and health and well-being.

The insights gained from its materiality assessments have been integral to shaping Unilever's business strategy. For example, recognizing the material issue of sustainable sourcing, Unilever committed to sourcing 100% of its agricultural raw materials sustainably by 2020. This commitment not only addressed environmental and social concerns but also secured long-term supply chain stability and opened up new markets.

Unilever's focused approach has led to significant achievements. The company reported a 50% reduction in waste associated with the disposal of its products and a significant reduction in CO_2 emissions. Furthermore, its sustainable living brands, which are closely aligned with the identified material issues, delivered more than 60% of the company's growth and grew at twice the rate of the rest of the business.

Unilever's experience highlights several key lessons in applying materiality:

- **Stakeholder Engagement is Crucial:** Regular and deep engagement helps ensure that the materiality assessment reflects a broad range of perspectives and is aligned with both external expectations and business priorities.

- **Integration into Business Strategy is Essential:** Materiality is not just a reporting tool but a strategic framework that should guide decision-making and resource allocation.

- **Transparency Builds Trust:** Unilever's transparent reporting on its progress, including areas where it has struggled, has built trust with consumers and stakeholders, enhancing its brand and business resilience.

Applying materiality comes with its challenges, including the need for a robust mechanism to gather and analyze stakeholder input and the requirement to balance diverse and sometimes competing interests. However, the opportunities outweigh these challenges by providing a clear path for sustainable growth. A well-executed materiality assessment enables companies to proactively address risks, innovate in product and service offerings, and strengthen stakeholder relationships.

Unilever's application of materiality serves as a compelling example for other organizations aiming to enhance their ESG impact. By prioritizing material issues and integrating them into their core business strategies, companies can not only drive meaningful change but also achieve sustainable success in an increasingly complex global market. This case study exemplifies how materiality, when strategically applied, can unlock significant opportunities for organizations committed to making a positive impact.

Exercise: Conducting a Materiality Assessment for Your Organization

This exercise is designed to guide leaders through the steps of conducting a materiality assessment, helping them to identify and prioritize the ESG issues that are most significant to their organization and its stakeholders. This process will assist in aligning sustainability efforts with business strategies, enhancing both organizational impact and stakeholder engagement.

Step 1: Define the Scope and Objectives

Scope: Determine the boundaries of your assessment—will it cover the entire organization or specific departments or product lines?

Objectives: Clarify what you aim to achieve with this assessment. Are you looking to update your sustainability strategy, enhance stakeholder relations, or improve compliance and reporting?

Step 2: Identify Key Stakeholders

Identify all relevant stakeholders who are affected by or can affect your organization's ESG issues. This group could include employees, customers, suppliers, local communities, investors, and regulators.

Step 3: Develop and Distribute Surveys

Create surveys tailored to each stakeholder group to gather insights on their perceptions of what ESG issues are most important. Ensure questions are open-ended where possible to capture a wide range of responses.

Step 4: Conduct Stakeholder Interviews and Focus Groups

In addition to surveys, conduct interviews and focus groups with key stakeholder representatives to dive deeper into specific issues or concerns. This qualitative data will provide context and depth to the survey results.

Step 5: Collect and Analyze Data

Gather all responses and analyze the data to identify which ESG issues are perceived as most critical by different stakeholder groups. Use a materiality matrix to map these issues based on their impact on the organization and their importance to stakeholders.

Step 6: Prioritize Material Issues

Based on the analysis, prioritize the issues that are both highly impactful on your organization's success and of high concern to your stakeholders. These are the areas where focused efforts will likely yield the most significant benefits.

Step 7: Validate Findings with Senior Management

Present your findings to senior management for validation and further input. This step ensures alignment with broader business objectives and secures executive buy-in for subsequent actions.

Step 8: Integrate into Strategy

Use the results of the materiality assessment to inform and update your organization's sustainability strategy. This should include setting specific, measurable goals for addressing each priority issue and integrating these goals into overall business operations and planning.

Step 9: Communicate Results

Transparently communicate what was found during the materiality assessment and what steps the organization plans to take as a result. This communication should be tailored to different stakeholder groups to ensure it is relevant and engaging.

Step 10: Establish a Review Process

Finally, set up a process for regularly reviewing and updating the materiality assessment. As stakeholder expectations shift and the business environment evolves, it will be crucial to reassess priorities and strategies.

This exercise not only guides leaders in conducting a thorough materiality assessment but also in interpreting and utilizing the results to drive meaningful change. The ability to identify and focus on material ESG issues is crucial for aligning sustainability initiatives with business strategies and for enhancing the long-term resilience and success of the organization.

Chapter 9: Frameworks for Purpose-Driven Leadership

In today's rapidly evolving world, the expectations placed on leaders have expanded significantly. Traditional leadership models, primarily focused on financial metrics and short-term gains, are increasingly seen as insufficient for addressing the complex challenges of the 21st century. Modern stakeholders—be they employees, customers, investors, or community members—demand transparency, sustainability, ethical conduct, and a clear commitment to societal impact from corporate leaders. This shift necessitates a new leadership paradigm that not only embraces these expectations but is also equipped to act upon them effectively.

In response to this need, this chapter introduces a comprehensive framework designed to integrate purpose and Environmental, Social, and Governance (ESG) considerations into leadership practices. This framework guides leaders in marrying their strategic goals with sustainable and ethical principles, ensuring that their organizations not only succeed financially but also contribute positively to society and the environment.

Purpose-driven leadership is defined by its commitment to a clear and meaningful purpose that goes beyond profit generation to include creating value for a broad range of stakeholders. This type of leadership is critical in today's business environment, where the impact of corporate actions on the community and the planet is as scrutinized as financial performance. The framework for purpose-driven leadership comprises several key components:

- Vision: Establishing a compelling vision that aligns with both the organization's long-term goals and its broader societal obligations. This vision serves as a guiding star for all strategic decisions and initiatives.

- Values: Core values that reflect the organization's ethical commitments and define the behaviors expected within the organization. These values must be deeply embedded in the organization's culture and consistently upheld by all, starting at the top.

- Culture: A culture that promotes sustainability, inclusiveness, and responsibility. Such a culture not only supports internal morale and engagement but also enhances the organization's reputation and appeal to external stakeholders.

- Strategy: Strategic planning that integrates ESG factors and aligns them with the organization's economic objectives. This involves setting clear, actionable goals that balance profit with purpose.

- Impact: Measuring and communicating the impact of the organization's actions on both financial performance and its contributions to societal goals. This requires robust mechanisms for tracking, reporting, and continuously improving the organization's social and environmental footprints.

Integrating purpose and ESG into leadership is not just about policy adjustments; it involves a fundamental shift in how leaders perceive their roles and responsibilities. Leaders must not only advocate for but also embody the principles of sustainability, ethics, and societal impact in their daily decisions and actions. This integration is achieved through continuous education, stakeholder engagement, and a commitment to transparency and accountability.

Leaders must ensure that purpose and ESG principles are not siloed in separate corporate social responsibility departments but are woven throughout all business operations and decision-making processes. This holistic integration can transform challenges into opportunities for innovation and competitive advantage, driving long-term sustainability and success.

Purpose-driven leadership requires a rethinking of traditional leadership models and a robust framework that supports leaders in navigating the complexities of modern business landscapes. This chapter sets the foundation for such a framework, offering leaders the tools they need to redefine success in an interconnected, interdependent world.

Embedding purpose and Environmental, Social, and Governance (ESG) considerations into the core of leadership practices requires strategic intent and thoughtful implementation. Leaders must demonstrate a genuine commitment to these principles, not just by endorsing ESG initiatives but by actively participating and integrating them into their decision-making processes. This involves incorporating ESG metrics alongside financial and operational metrics to ensure comprehensive evaluations in every aspect of the business.

Continuous education on sustainability and ethical practices is essential for all employees, particularly management, to ensure that the workforce is knowledgeable and motivated to implement these principles effectively. Moreover, leaders play a crucial role in championing sustainability and ethical practices within the organization. They must ensure these practices are integral to the organization's overall strategy and success, embodying the behaviors they expect to see throughout the organization and dedicating resources specifically to sustainability and ethics initiatives.

Leadership involvement extends to developing and enforcing policies that support sustainable and ethical operations, which should be well-communicated and integrated into the daily operations of the company. Regular stakeholder engagement is also critical; by regularly interacting with stakeholders to gather insights and feedback on the organization's ESG efforts, leaders can ensure that their strategies remain aligned with both stakeholder expectations and societal values.

To align an organization's strategy with purpose and ESG principles, it is important to integrate these considerations into the strategic planning process from the outset. Leaders should set clear, measurable goals related to purpose and ESG that align with the broader strategic objectives of the organization. Every department and function should align with the organization's ESG goals, necessitating changes across various aspects of operations, from procurement and manufacturing to HR and marketing, to reflect the organization's commitment to its purpose and ESG principles.

Developing a robust system for tracking and reporting ESG performance against set goals is crucial. Regular internal and external reporting of these findings not only holds the organization accountable to its commitments but also builds trust with stakeholders. Additionally, establishing mechanisms for continuous improvement in ESG practices encourages innovation and allows for revising strategies and goals as needed based on performance and changing external conditions.

By adopting these comprehensive strategies, leaders can ensure that purpose and ESG considerations drive the organization's culture and operations forward, creating a resilient, sustainable, and ethically driven business.

Cultivating a culture that supports purpose-driven leadership and integrates Environmental, Social, and Governance (ESG) principles effectively requires deliberate actions and consistent effort from organizational leaders. This cultural shift is essential for ensuring that the organization not only achieves its sustainability goals but also fosters a workplace environment where employees are engaged and motivated by a shared sense of purpose.

Creating a purpose-driven culture begins with clear communication from the top. Leaders must articulate the organization's purpose and sustainability goals in a way that resonates with all employees, making the purpose tangible and relevant to everyone's roles within the company. This involves not just stating the purpose but demonstrating how it connects to daily operations and individual responsibilities. By doing so, leaders can help employees see how their work contributes to larger organizational objectives, enhancing their sense of value and engagement.

Engaging employees in meaningful ways is crucial for embedding a purpose-driven culture. This can be achieved through regular discussions, workshops, and training sessions that not only educate employees about the importance of sustainability and ethical practices but also invite their input on how these goals can be met. Encouraging employees to contribute ideas and solutions fosters a sense of ownership and commitment to the organization's purpose.

Aligning recognition and reward systems with the achievement of purpose and ESG goals reinforces the importance of these efforts. When employees are recognized and rewarded for behaviors that support sustainability and ethical practices, it sends a powerful message about what the organization values. This can significantly enhance motivation and buy-in from employees across all levels of the organization.

Stakeholder engagement is another critical aspect of building a purpose-driven culture. By involving customers, suppliers, investors, and the local community in the organization's sustainability initiatives, leaders can create a broader sense of commitment and accountability to the purpose. This external engagement not only helps in refining the organization's strategies based on stakeholder feedback but also strengthens the organization's reputation and influence in the wider community.

Developing and nurturing a purpose-driven culture is an ongoing process that requires consistent leadership commitment, active employee engagement, and meaningful stakeholder interactions. By focusing on these areas, organizations can create an environment that supports purpose-driven leadership and effective ESG integration, ultimately leading to sustained organizational success and a positive impact on society.

Effectively measuring and communicating the impact of purpose-driven leadership and ESG initiatives are essential components of maintaining transparency and accountability within any organization. Establishing clear metrics and indicators aligned with ESG goals lays the groundwork for these efforts, beginning with setting baselines and specific targets to gauge progress. Regular data collection, encompassing both quantitative and qualitative assessments, then feeds into a comprehensive analysis of how well the initiatives are performing against these established benchmarks.

To convey the findings from these measurements, organizations should adopt integrated reporting practices. These reports, which blend financial and non-financial data, offer a holistic view of how ESG efforts are meshing with broader business objectives, thereby showcasing the tangible benefits of sustainable practices. The communication strategy must extend beyond mere reporting. Transparency is crucial; organizations need to be open about both their successes and the challenges they encounter. This honesty not only builds trust but also enhances credibility with stakeholders, showing a commitment to real progress and integrity in sustainability efforts.

Frequent updates are necessary to keep stakeholders engaged and informed. These should be disseminated through a variety of channels—annual reports, updates on the company's website, press releases, and direct communications during stakeholder meetings. By employing diverse platforms, including social media, webinars, and traditional media, the organization ensures that its message resonates across a broad audience spectrum.

Storytelling can be a powerful tool in this communication strategy. By framing ESG achievements and obstacles within compelling narratives—such as personal stories from employees or impacts on the community—organizations can make the complex or abstract elements of their initiatives more relatable and easier to understand.

Stakeholder feedback on these communications should be actively encouraged. This feedback not only helps gauge the effectiveness of the messaging but also fosters a dialogic relationship with stakeholders, where suggestions and concerns can lead to improvements in ESG strategies. Through meticulous measurement and dynamic communication, organizations can enhance their accountability and reinforce their commitment to purpose-driven leadership. This approach not only strengthens stakeholder trust but also supports long-term success and sustainability in an increasingly conscientious business environment.

Overcoming the barriers to implementing purpose-driven leadership and integrating Environmental, Social, and Governance (ESG) principles requires navigating several common obstacles that can hinder these efforts. Among these, resistance to change within the organization is notably significant. Employees and even managers, accustomed to traditional operational methods, might view new initiatives that prioritize sustainability alongside profitability with skepticism. This resistance often arises from a misunderstanding of the benefits these practices offer or fear that changes might disrupt established processes and roles.

Another pervasive challenge is the absence of clear direction and robust commitment from the top leadership. Purpose-driven leadership demands explicit articulation of the organization's purpose and strategic ESG goals. Without strong leadership endorsement, these initiatives may lack the necessary authority and resources for effective implementation. Additionally, measuring the impact of these initiatives poses its own set of challenges. Traditional financial metrics do not fully capture the broader value created by ESG initiatives, complicating the task of communicating their benefits both internally and externally.

To address these challenges effectively, organizations must adopt a multi-faceted strategic approach. Enhancing understanding and buy-in across all levels of the organization is crucial. This can be achieved through education, transparent communication, and by sharing success stories and case studies that illustrate the practical benefits and potential for positive impact. Regular training sessions, workshops, and seminars can help demystify ESG principles and demonstrate how they align with the business's core objectives, building broad-based support.

Leadership commitment is also essential. Leaders must not only verbally endorse ESG initiatives but also actively participate in them. This includes being visible in their commitment, discussing the organization's ESG goals and progress through internal communications, and public engagements. Establishing clear metrics and regular reporting is another critical strategy. Organizations should adopt or develop comprehensive frameworks that measure social and environmental impact alongside financial performance, integrating these metrics into public disclosures to enhance transparency and accountability.

Cultivating a supportive culture is fundamental. It involves more than issuing top-down directives; it requires creating an environment where every employee feels empowered and aligned with the company's purpose. Recognizing and rewarding efforts that advance ESG goals and integrating these principles into the company's core values and operational procedures can significantly reinforce this culture. Maintaining momentum in ESG initiatives demands a commitment to continuous improvement. This includes regular reviews of strategies and practices, staying informed about new developments in sustainability and corporate responsibility, and being receptive to feedback from all stakeholders. By understanding and strategically addressing these barriers, organizations can enhance their ability to integrate ESG principles effectively, driving not only business success but also contributing to a more sustainable and equitable global business environment.

As we conclude our exploration of purpose-driven leadership, it becomes increasingly clear that this framework is not just beneficial but essential for addressing the complex challenges of today's world. The integration of Environmental, Social, and Governance (ESG) principles with a firm commitment to purpose helps ensure that organizations do more than just succeed financially; they also play a pivotal role in driving societal progress and environmental stewardship.

The journey through various models and examples of purpose-driven leadership underscores the transformative power of aligning organizational strategies with broader societal and environmental goals. This alignment not only mitigates risks and enhances brand reputation but also opens up new avenues for innovation and growth. As leaders, embracing this framework means committing to continuous improvement and striving to understand the evolving dynamics of our global ecosystem.

Leaders are encouraged to take proactive steps toward fully integrating purpose and ESG into their leadership approaches. This involves embedding sustainability into the core business operations, ensuring that every decision is weighed not just for its immediate benefits but for its long-term impact on the planet and society. It also requires cultivating an organizational culture that values ethical conduct, inclusivity, and responsibility, empowering every employee to contribute to the organization's purpose-driven goals.

As we look to the future, leaders have the opportunity—and the responsibility—to be pioneers in creating a sustainable, ethical, and purposeful future. This call to action is not just about making incremental changes but about leading a fundamental shift in how businesses operate and how they perceive their role in the world. By championing purpose-driven leadership, leaders can ensure that their organizations not only thrive but also contribute positively to the world, creating a legacy of impact and resilience.

Leading with purpose is about envisioning a better future and actively working towards it. It is about setting an example for integrity, innovation, and inclusiveness in all aspects of business operations. As we move forward, let this framework guide your strategies, your decisions, and your actions. Let it inspire you to build not just a more successful business but a better world. For leaders ready to embrace this challenge, the path ahead is promising, filled with opportunities to make a significant difference for this generation and those to come.

Case Study: IKEA on Purpose-Driven Leadership

IKEA, the Swedish furniture giant, stands as a prominent example of purpose-driven leadership, recognized globally for its dedication to sustainability and environmental stewardship. Since its inception, IKEA has integrated purpose into every facet of its operations, which is particularly evident in its approach to product design, materials sourcing, and community involvement.

Under the leadership of its visionary executives, IKEA has set forth an ambitious agenda to become a fully circular and climate-positive business by 2030. This commitment is reflected in its wide-ranging sustainability strategies, which include phasing out single-use plastics, investing in renewable energy projects, and designing products with reusability, repairability, and recyclability in mind. These initiatives are not mere add-ons but are central to IKEA's business model, illustrating the company's integration of purpose into its core operations.

IKEA's journey has not been without challenges. One of the significant hurdles has been maintaining cost-effectiveness while transitioning to more sustainable practices. The company has tackled this by innovating in its supply chain and manufacturing processes, often opting to absorb higher costs to ensure that its products remain sustainable without compromising affordability for its customers.

Another challenge involves supply chain transparency and ensuring that all suppliers adhere to the same high standards of environmental and social responsibility that IKEA sets for itself. To address this, IKEA has implemented rigorous supplier standards and regular audits to maintain compliance with its corporate values, enhancing the sustainability of its extensive global supply network.

The impact of IKEA's purpose-driven leadership is substantial, offering valuable lessons on the scalability of sustainable practices in a global retail operation. The company's commitment to transparency has been crucial; openly sharing its goals, progress, and setbacks has not only built trust with consumers but also established IKEA as a leader in corporate responsibility. This transparency is complemented by proactive stakeholder engagement, where feedback is actively solicited and used to refine strategies and operations.

IKEA's approach to embedding sustainability into its culture involves not only setting ambitious external goals but also fostering an internal ethos that encourages employees at all levels to participate in its sustainability mission. This inclusive culture has fueled innovation and motivated the workforce, further driving the company's sustainability goals forward. IKEA's adherence to purpose-driven leadership has not only enhanced its market position but also demonstrated that integrating ethical and sustainable practices into the core business strategy can drive substantial business growth and societal impact. IKEA's efforts show that with strategic commitment and innovative execution, companies can achieve impressive sustainability outcomes while remaining competitive in the global market. This case study serves as an inspiration for other companies aiming to align their operations with broader environmental and social objectives.

Exercise: Applying the Purpose-Driven Leadership Framework

This guided exercise is designed to help leaders apply the purpose-driven leadership framework within their own organizations, identifying areas of strength and opportunities for further integration of purpose and ESG principles.

Objective: To assess and enhance the alignment of your organization's leadership practices with purpose-driven and ESG principles.

Materials Needed:

Purpose-Driven Leadership Framework Checklist
ESG Integration Worksheet
Stakeholder Feedback Forms
Strategic Alignment Map

Step 1: Self-Assessment

Begin by reflecting on your current leadership practices. Using the Purpose-Driven Leadership Framework Checklist, rate your organization on areas such as ethical leadership, stakeholder engagement, environmental stewardship, social responsibility, and governance. Identify strengths where your organization already aligns well with purpose-driven and ESG principles.

Step 2: Stakeholder Engagement

Distribute Stakeholder Feedback Forms to a diverse group of stakeholders, including employees, customers, suppliers, and community partners. Ask for their perceptions of your organization's strengths and areas for improvement in relation to purpose and ESG practices. Gather and analyze the feedback to understand external perceptions and expectations.

Step 3: Opportunity Identification

Using the feedback and your self-assessment, fill out the ESG Integration Worksheet. List down the areas of strength and identify key opportunities where further integration of purpose and ESG principles could be beneficial. Prioritize these opportunities based on their potential impact on both the organization and its stakeholders.

Step 4: Strategic Planning

Develop specific, actionable plans for each identified opportunity. Use the Strategic Alignment Map to ensure that these plans align with your organization's overall strategy and purpose. Define clear objectives, assign responsibilities, and set timelines for each action item.

Step 5: Implementation

Begin implementing the plans, focusing on quick wins first to build momentum and gain wider organizational support. Ensure that each department or team understands their role in these initiatives and has the resources they need to succeed.

Step 6: Monitoring and Reporting

Establish regular monitoring processes to track the progress of the implementation against the set goals. Schedule periodic review meetings with stakeholders to discuss progress, share successes, and adjust plans as necessary.

Step 7: Integration and Continuous Improvement

Integrate the insights gained from this exercise into regular business operations and decision-making processes. Commit to continuous improvement by revisiting the Purpose-Driven Leadership Framework annually and adjusting your strategies to meet new challenges and stakeholder expectations.

This exercise is designed to make the principles of purpose-driven leadership tangible and actionable within your organization. By methodically assessing and enhancing alignment with these principles, you can ensure that your leadership not only drives business success but also makes a positive impact on society and the environment.

Chapter 10: Communicating Your ESG Journey

Effective communication plays a pivotal role in the success of an organization's Environmental, Social, and Governance (ESG) initiatives. It is not only about articulating what the company is doing to address ESG concerns but also about why these efforts matter. This chapter explores the importance of transparent and impactful communication in sharing an organization's ESG journey, highlighting how well-crafted messages can build trust and engage a broad spectrum of stakeholders.

The role of transparency in ESG communication cannot be overstated. Openness about both successes and challenges not only fosters trust but also humanizes the organization's efforts, making them more relatable and understandable to its audience. Moreover, storytelling emerges as a powerful tool in ESG communication, providing a means to connect emotionally with stakeholders, from investors and customers to employees and community members. Well-told stories can vividly illustrate the impact of the organization's ESG initiatives, bringing abstract concepts to life and demonstrating tangible benefits.

Effective ESG reporting is grounded in several key principles: clarity, accuracy, and consistency. These principles ensure that the information provided is not only reliable and comprehensive but also accessible to stakeholders with varying levels of expertise. Clarity involves presenting information in a straightforward manner, free from jargon and ambiguity. Accuracy is crucial for maintaining credibility; it requires diligent data collection and validation to ensure that all reported information is correct and verifiable. Consistency in reporting, both in terms of the metrics used and the frequency of communication, helps stakeholders track progress over time, providing a clear view of the organization's evolution in addressing ESG issues.

Adhering to recognized ESG reporting standards and frameworks is also significant. Standards such as those set by the Global Reporting Initiative (GRI), the Sustainability Accounting Standards Board (SASB), and the Task Force on Climate-related Financial Disclosures (TCFD) provide guidelines that help ensure the credibility and comparability of ESG reports. Utilizing these frameworks not only enhances the organization's accountability but also aligns its reporting practices with global benchmarks, facilitating easier assessment and comparison by external parties.

The art of ESG storytelling is about transforming raw data and strategic initiatives into compelling narratives that resonate with a diverse array of stakeholders. This approach allows an organization to communicate not just the what and the how of its activities, but, crucially, the why. Storytelling can vividly showcase an organization's purpose, values, and impact on society and the environment, making the intangible aspects of ESG efforts tangible and relatable.

Effective storytelling in ESG involves highlighting specific examples of how the organization's efforts have led to meaningful change. This might include stories about how sustainable practices have improved community well-being, how governance reforms have enhanced operational transparency, or how social initiatives have enriched employee lives. These stories serve to contextualize the data, giving it depth and emotional relevance that can inspire stakeholders and reinforce the organization's commitment to its values.

In addition to crafting compelling narratives, engaging stakeholders through transparent communication is critical. This involves a deep understanding of the different information needs of various stakeholder groups. Investors might require detailed data on how ESG efforts contribute to financial performance, while customers might be more interested in understanding how these practices affect product quality and environmental impact. Employees, on the other hand, might focus on how ESG initiatives create a safer and more fulfilling work environment.

Identifying these needs allows organizations to tailor their communication strategies effectively. It's also essential to leverage various communication channels to ensure these messages reach their intended audiences. Traditional annual reports, sustainability updates on the company website, social media posts, newsletters, and face-to-face meetings all play a role. Each channel has its strengths and using them in combination can expand reach and enhance engagement. For instance, social media can be used to share ongoing initiatives and day-to-day actions, making the organization's efforts more visible and immediate. In contrast, formal reports might provide a more comprehensive and detailed account of progress and future directions, appealing to those who seek deeper understanding and analysis.

By integrating these strategies—tailoring the narrative to meet diverse stakeholder needs and choosing the appropriate channels for communication—organizations can ensure that their ESG storytelling is not only heard but also felt and acted upon. This holistic approach not only informs but also engages stakeholders, drawing them into a shared journey towards sustainability and responsible governance. Through this dynamic interaction, organizations can build trust, foster loyalty, and drive collective action towards a more sustainable and ethical future.

Leveraging digital platforms for ESG communication has become increasingly crucial as organizations strive to reach a broader and more connected audience. Digital media, including websites, social media platforms, and even dedicated ESG portals, provide dynamic tools for disseminating information and engaging with stakeholders in real-time. These platforms serve multifaceted roles: websites act as hubs for detailed ESG reports and updates, while social media allows for more frequent interaction and helps humanize the ESG narrative by sharing stories, milestones, and challenges as they happen. This real-time sharing fosters a sense of community and shared purpose among followers, enhancing stakeholder engagement.

To maximize the impact of digital platforms, several strategies should be considered. Maintaining a consistent message across all platforms is crucial, as regular updates and consistent terminology help build a recognizable and reliable voice that stakeholders come to trust. Utilizing compelling visuals and multimedia, such as infographics, videos, and interactive content, can significantly enhance engagement levels. These formats are particularly effective in simplifying complex data, making it accessible to a broader audience.

Digital platforms should also be interactive, offering opportunities for stakeholders to engage with the content through Q&A sessions, live discussions, and polls. This two-way communication makes stakeholders feel heard and involved in the organization's ESG journey. Monitoring these interactions using analytics tools is essential to understand what types of content generate the most engagement, guiding future content creation and ensuring that the organization remains responsive to stakeholder interests and concerns.

Ensuring accessibility is another critical aspect, making sure all digital ESG communications are accessible to people with disabilities, which includes providing text alternatives for non-text content, ensuring website compatibility with screen readers, and using clear and simple language.

Digital platforms also play a crucial role in crisis management, allowing organizations to quickly communicate their response to any ESG-related issues. Proactive and transparent communication during crises helps maintain stakeholder trust and demonstrates the organization's commitment to its ESG principles, even in challenging times.

By effectively utilizing digital platforms, organizations can not only extend their reach but also deepen their interactions with stakeholders, creating more meaningful and sustained engagements. As digital media continues to evolve, so too will the strategies for using these tools to communicate an organization's ESG efforts, making it an ever more integral part of the ESG reporting and communication landscape.

Overcoming challenges in ESG communication is critical to ensuring that the efforts in sustainability and governance are both understood and trusted by stakeholders. Common pitfalls such as information overload and greenwashing can undermine the credibility and impact of an organization's ESG initiatives. Information overload occurs when stakeholders are bombarded with too much data, making it difficult for them to discern what is most important. Greenwashing — the practice of making misleading claims about the environmental benefits of a product, service, or technology — can severely damage a brand's reputation and trust with stakeholders.

To navigate these challenges, organizations must adopt strategic approaches to streamline and authenticate their communications. Achieving clarity and credibility involves focusing on the quality rather than the quantity of information. This means carefully selecting which data to highlight based on what is most relevant and impactful to the intended audience. It is also crucial to provide context for the data, explaining not just the numbers but also what they mean in terms of the organization's broader ESG goals and impact. To combat greenwashing, transparency is key. Organizations should avoid making broad claims that cannot be substantiated by specific data or third-party verification. Instead, they should link their ESG claims to recognized standards, certifications, or independent audits that can verify their assertions. This approach not only enhances credibility but also demonstrates a genuine commitment to ESG principles, rather than a superficial attempt to appear sustainable.

Simplifying the presentation of ESG data can also help in overcoming information overload. This can be achieved by using clear, concise language and visual aids like charts and graphs to make complex information more accessible and easier to understand. Regular training for employees on how to communicate ESG efforts effectively can also ensure that everyone in the organization can articulate these points clearly and confidently.

Another effective strategy is to engage stakeholders in a dialogue about ESG efforts and progress. This two-way communication allows organizations to gather feedback on what stakeholders find most valuable and where they may have concerns or need more information. It also helps to build and maintain a dialogue that can keep stakeholders informed and involved over time, fostering a deeper connection and alignment with the organization's ESG objectives.

By addressing these challenges head-on with clear strategies and a commitment to transparency, organizations can ensure that their ESG communication is clear, credible, and impactful. This not only enhances stakeholder trust and engagement but also strengthens the organization's overall ESG strategy, driving meaningful change and delivering on the promise of sustainability and responsibility.

It should now be clear that effective communication plays a critical role in enhancing an organization's Environmental, Social, and Governance (ESG) initiatives. Through clear, credible, and impactful messaging, organizations can not only inform but also inspire their stakeholders, fostering a deeper understanding and commitment to sustainability goals.

The importance of transparency cannot be overstated in the context of ESG communication. It is the bedrock upon which trust is built and maintained between an organization and its stakeholders. Transparency involves not just the sharing of successes but also openly discussing challenges and setbacks. This honesty helps stakeholders understand the complexities of implementing ESG initiatives and reassures them of the organization's commitment to genuine improvement.

The power of storytelling in ESG communication helps bring abstract concepts and large datasets to life. By articulating how individual actions and strategies impact the broader community and environment, organizations can make their ESG efforts relatable and tangible. Storytelling not only engages the audience emotionally but also highlights the organization's purpose and values in a powerful and memorable way.

Stakeholder engagement is another crucial element. By actively involving customers, employees, suppliers, and the broader community in their ESG journey, organizations can ensure that their strategies are responsive to stakeholder needs and aligned with broader societal expectations. Engaging stakeholders through regular updates, interactive platforms, and direct dialogues ensures that the ESG narrative remains dynamic and relevant.

Strengthening your ESG narrative is an ongoing process that requires attention, creativity, and strategic thinking. Leaders are encouraged to continuously refine and amplify their ESG narratives, integrating transparency, storytelling, and stakeholder engagement into their communication efforts. This not only enhances the organization's credibility and reputation but also contributes significantly to its sustainable and responsible business practices.

As organizations look to the future, the call to action is clear: prioritize and enhance your ESG communications as a fundamental aspect of your leadership strategy. By doing so, you can ensure that your organization not only meets the challenges of today but also leads the way in building a sustainable and equitable future.

Case Study: Effective ESG Communication in Action - LEGO Group

The LEGO Group, renowned for its iconic building blocks, has also built a strong reputation for its commitment to environmental sustainability and social responsibility. The company's approach to communicating its ESG journey serves as an exemplary model for how strategic messaging can enhance stakeholder engagement and foster a positive corporate image.

LEGO has developed a comprehensive ESG communication strategy that centers around transparency, engaging storytelling, and proactive stakeholder interaction. This strategy involves a series of detailed sustainability reports that LEGO makes available to the public, providing an in-depth look at the company's goals and progress in areas such as reducing carbon footprint, ethical supply chain practices, and community involvement. These reports are complemented by regular updates via the company's website and social media channels, ensuring that stakeholders can follow LEGO's journey in real-time.

Storytelling plays a pivotal role in LEGO's ESG communication. The company often shares stories about its efforts to create sustainable products, such as its initiative to manufacture LEGO bricks from plant-based materials. These stories are told through various media, including videos that depict the research and development process, interviews with product designers, and insights from sustainability experts within the company. By presenting these narratives, LEGO not only informs its audience but also connects with them on an emotional level, highlighting the impact of their sustainability efforts on the environment and future generations.

LEGO's proactive stakeholder engagement is another key component of its ESG strategy. The company actively seeks input from consumers, especially focusing on how its products and practices align with their values. LEGO also engages with environmental organizations to bolster its sustainability initiatives, ensuring that its strategies are informed by the latest research and best practices in environmental stewardship.

The impact of LEGO's ESG communication strategies has been overwhelmingly positive. The company has observed increased consumer loyalty, particularly among environmentally conscious customers who value LEGO's commitment to sustainability. Moreover, LEGO's transparent and engaging communication has strengthened its relationships with suppliers and partners, who are keen to align themselves with a company that prioritizes responsible business practices.

LEGO's success in ESG communication underscores several valuable lessons for other organizations. An integrated communication strategy that combines detailed reporting, compelling storytelling, and active stakeholder engagement can significantly enhance the visibility and impact of a company's ESG efforts. Consistent and clear communication across multiple platforms ensures that stakeholders receive a unified message about the organization's commitment to sustainability. Furthermore, incorporating feedback from stakeholders not only refines ESG strategies but also fosters a sense of community and shared purpose.

The LEGO Group demonstrates that effective ESG communication is crucial for not just articulating a company's sustainability journey but also for embedding these principles into the fabric of the corporate identity. By adopting a strategic approach to ESG communication, companies can ensure their initiatives are both visible and impactful, paving the way for a sustainable and responsible business landscape.

Exercise: Creating an ESG Report Outline for Your Organization

This guided exercise is designed to help leaders draft an effective outline for their organization's Environmental, Social, and Governance (ESG) report. The goal is to create a document that not only details key areas of impact, achievements, and goals but also incorporates storytelling elements to make the report both engaging and informative.

Objective: To produce a structured and compelling ESG report that clearly communicates the organization's sustainability efforts, progress, and future goals to stakeholders.

Materials Needed:

ESG performance data
Stakeholder feedback
Previous ESG reports (if available)
Template for report outline
Guidelines on storytelling in business communication

Step 1: Define the Scope and Audience

Start by defining the scope of your ESG report. Decide whether the report will cover all areas of ESG or focus on specific aspects such as environmental impact or social responsibility. Identify your primary audience. Are you writing for investors, customers, employees, or regulatory bodies? Understanding your audience will help tailor the content to their interests and needs.

Step 2: Gather Information

Collect all relevant data on your organization's ESG performance. This includes quantitative data like carbon footprint measurements and qualitative insights such as employee well-being programs. Review feedback from stakeholders to understand their concerns and priorities. This input can help highlight areas that need more detailed coverage in the report.

Step 3: Draft the Report Structure

- Begin with an executive summary that captures the essence of your ESG efforts and achievements in a succinct manner.
- Organize the main body of the report into sections based on the ESG areas you are covering. Common sections include:
- Environmental Impact: Detail initiatives like waste reduction, recycling programs, and energy efficiency improvements.
- Social Responsibility: Describe efforts in community engagement, diversity and inclusion programs, and employee welfare.
- Governance: Explain governance structures, ethical standards, and compliance measures.

Step 4: Incorporate Storytelling

Within each section, use storytelling to bring data to life. This might involve sharing a case study of a successful community project or a story about how a new governance policy was developed. Use visuals such as charts, graphs, and photos to help tell these stories. Visuals can illustrate progress over time or show the real-world impact of your initiatives.

Step 5: Highlight Achievements and Set Future Goals

Clearly outline what the organization has achieved in the past year. Be specific about the goals met and the impact created. Discuss future goals and the strategies planned to achieve them. This not only shows ambition but also accountability, as stakeholders can look forward to tracking your progress.

Step 6: Review and Revise

Once the initial draft is complete, review the report for clarity, accuracy, and engagement. Ensure that the storytelling elements are effectively integrated and that the data presented is accurate.

Solicit feedback from different departments to ensure that all information is comprehensive and reflects the organization's efforts across the board.

Finalize the report by revising it based on the feedback received. Ensure that the final document is professionally presented and accessible, keeping in mind the primary audience. The completed ESG report should not only inform stakeholders about your organization's sustainability journey but also engage and inspire them by clearly demonstrating your commitment to making a positive impact on society and the environment.

Chapter 11: Leading with Purpose: Transforming Challenges into Opportunities

In today's rapidly changing world, marked by environmental crises, social inequalities, and economic volatility, the need for purpose-driven leadership has never been more critical. Such leaders are distinguished not only by their ability to achieve business success but also by their commitment to addressing global challenges through Environmental, Social, and Governance (ESG) initiatives. The potential of purposeful leadership extends beyond merely navigating these challenges; it involves transforming them into opportunities for growth, innovation, and significant positive impact.

Purpose-driven leaders view the complexities of the modern world as catalysts for improvement and innovation within their organizations. They leverage ESG initiatives to drive change, enhance sustainability, and build resilience, thereby not only contributing to the welfare of the planet and its people but also securing a competitive edge in the marketplace. By doing so, they turn potential threats into avenues for development and differentiation.

Leaders are uniquely positioned to advocate for and implement ESG initiatives within their organizations. They have the influence to shape strategic priorities and the authority to allocate resources towards sustainable practices. More importantly, they have the capability to inspire and mobilize entire organizations towards a shared vision of responsible business conduct.

To effectively champion ESG initiatives, purpose-driven leaders must first ensure that these initiatives are aligned with the organization's core mission and values. This alignment helps in integrating ESG seamlessly into everyday business operations and decision-making processes, making sustainability a part of the organizational DNA rather than a peripheral concern.

Leaders must also be adept at communicating the value of these initiatives to all stakeholders, from employees and shareholders to customers and community members. This involves clear, consistent messaging that connects ESG efforts with tangible benefits, such as operational efficiencies, market growth, and enhanced corporate reputation. By doing so, leaders can cultivate a culture of sustainability throughout the organization, where every stakeholder feels engaged and motivated to contribute. These purpose driven leaders act as role models, demonstrating a personal commitment to ESG values. This can be seen in their decision-making, their public statements, and their willingness to be held accountable for the organization's environmental and social impacts. Their example sets the standard for behavior within the organization and fosters a culture of integrity and responsibility.

As the global landscape continues to evolve, the call for purpose-driven leadership becomes increasingly urgent. Leaders who embrace this call and effectively champion ESG initiatives not only transform challenges into opportunities for their organizations but also contribute to the broader goal of sustainable development. By leading with purpose, they ensure that their organizations do well by doing good, creating enduring value for both their stakeholders and society at large.

Implementing ESG initiatives often comes with obstacles like resistance to change, resource constraints, and lack of awareness. Resistance often emerges when employees and other stakeholders are comfortable with existing ways of doing things, viewing new ESG measures as disruptive. Resource constraints also play a significant role, as budgetary limits can hinder investment in sustainable practices. Moreover, a lack of awareness about the value of ESG integration means that not everyone appreciates the long-term benefits of such initiatives.

Purpose-driven leaders address these obstacles by actively engaging stakeholders to help them see the value of ESG initiatives. Open and transparent communication, combined with listening to concerns and adjusting strategies, accordingly, fosters an environment where people feel heard and understood. Leaders also emphasize how aligning with ESG goals can enhance long-term business performance, creating a compelling narrative that resonates across all levels of the organization.

Leaders leverage data and evidence to show how ESG initiatives can drive efficiencies and open new revenue streams. For instance, data demonstrating the cost savings from energy efficiency or the market growth potential of sustainable products can motivate even the most reluctant stakeholders. Evidence-based decision-making strengthens the case for ESG integration, making it more tangible and relatable.

Creating a culture of innovation and resilience is another crucial strategy. When employees are encouraged to think creatively about ESG challenges and are rewarded for their contributions, they become active participants in finding solutions. Leaders can nurture this culture by celebrating wins, whether small or significant, and by framing failures as learning opportunities rather than setbacks. This approach empowers teams to embrace ESG objectives with optimism and adaptability.

By combining stakeholder engagement, data-driven advocacy, and an innovative culture, purpose-driven leaders can successfully overcome obstacles to ESG implementation. They turn potential hurdles into stepping stones, driving their organizations forward while building a foundation for sustainable success.

Leading transformative change through the lens of ESG requires a careful and strategic approach that aligns initiatives with organizational strategy and values. It begins with a deep understanding of the company's core purpose and long-term vision, ensuring that ESG initiatives are not just add-ons but integral to achieving broader organizational goals. Leaders need to translate this vision into a strategic framework where ESG considerations are embedded in every aspect of the business.

To align these initiatives effectively, it's crucial to involve key stakeholders early in the process. Engaging employees, customers, investors, and community members in meaningful dialogue ensures their perspectives are considered, fostering a sense of ownership and shared purpose. This engagement helps identify the ESG issues most material to the organization, providing a clear focus for where to direct resources and efforts.

Once the priorities are set, leaders should develop a clear plan that outlines specific, measurable goals. These goals should align with the organization's broader strategic objectives while also pushing the business toward ambitious, purpose-driven outcomes. Regularly communicating progress keeps everyone aligned and reinforces the message that ESG initiatives are central to the organization's mission.

Leaders should also ensure that ESG principles permeate the organization's culture and operations. This means integrating sustainability goals into daily processes, incentivizing behaviors that support these goals, and holding teams accountable for their contributions. Developing training programs and knowledge-sharing platforms can further reinforce the importance of ESG and empower employees to incorporate these principles into their work. Furthermore, it's essential to remain flexible and adaptive. As market trends and societal expectations evolve, the organization must be willing to recalibrate its ESG strategy to stay relevant and impactful. This agility enables the business to navigate challenges and capitalize on new opportunities, ensuring that the transformative change achieved is both enduring and resilient.

Leading transformative change with ESG is a continuous journey requiring a strong strategic foundation, a collaborative culture, and a willingness to adapt. When executed well, it positions organizations not only to meet their sustainability goals but also to thrive in a world increasingly shaped by environmental and social concerns.

Creating a supportive ecosystem for ESG initiatives is essential for their success, as it involves cultivating an environment within and beyond the organization that encourages collaboration, learning, and shared goals. Internally, this ecosystem starts with strong leadership and a culture that prioritizes ESG principles. Leaders must clearly communicate the importance of these initiatives to all levels of the organization, ensuring that each department understands its role in achieving ESG goals. They should foster a culture where innovation and responsibility thrive, where employees are encouraged to contribute ideas and solutions that align with these principles.

A supportive ecosystem also requires robust internal structures that facilitate the seamless integration of ESG into daily operations. This could include cross-departmental working groups to coordinate efforts, regular training to keep employees informed about best practices, and transparent reporting mechanisms that track progress and celebrate successes.

Externally, building partnerships, alliances, and networks can amplify the impact of ESG initiatives. Collaborating with other businesses, nonprofits, industry groups, and governmental organizations creates a web of support that accelerates learning and problem-solving. Partnerships with nonprofits can help address social challenges more effectively by combining resources and expertise. Industry alliances can facilitate the sharing of best practices and standardize ESG benchmarks, while engagement with policymakers can help shape regulations that encourage sustainable practices.

These external relationships can also provide organizations with a broader perspective on emerging trends and potential challenges, enabling them to stay agile and ahead of the curve. For instance, participating in cross-sector networks allows businesses to benchmark their progress against industry standards and gain insights into innovative practices that could be adapted to their strategies.

In building this ecosystem, transparency and accountability are crucial. Organizations should be open about their ESG challenges and progress, inviting stakeholders to provide constructive feedback and hold them accountable. This builds trust and strengthens relationships, ensuring that the entire ecosystem is aligned and working toward common goals.

Creating a supportive ecosystem for ESG initiatives is about mobilizing both internal and external resources to foster collaboration, innovation, and accountability. With this foundation, organizations are better equipped to navigate challenges, amplify their impact, and drive meaningful progress toward a sustainable future.

Innovation plays a crucial role in propelling ESG initiatives forward, offering transformative approaches that turn challenges into opportunities. Leaders who embrace innovation in their ESG strategies can find creative solutions that not only address current issues but also lay the groundwork for long-term sustainability and growth.

One prominent example of this is the use of artificial intelligence (AI) and data analytics to enhance supply chain transparency. Traditionally, supply chain monitoring has been a laborious and opaque process, often leading to inefficiencies and ethical lapses. By leveraging AI, organizations can analyze vast amounts of data in real time, identifying risks and inefficiencies throughout their supply chains. This approach helps companies source materials more responsibly, minimize waste, and ensure ethical labor practices are followed.

Another innovative approach is the use of blockchain technology to improve traceability and trust in sustainable sourcing. Blockchain's immutable ledger system enables organizations to track products from their origin to the consumer, ensuring that every step in the supply chain aligns with ESG standards. For instance, coffee producers can guarantee that their beans are sourced ethically, while fashion brands can verify the origin and production conditions of their textiles.

In the realm of social impact, some organizations have harnessed the power of gamification to engage employees in their ESG efforts. By creating interactive platforms where employees can participate in sustainability challenges and receive rewards for their efforts, companies foster a culture of participation and collective responsibility. This approach not only raises awareness but also encourages proactive behavior change.

Embracing circular economy principles has emerged as a significant innovation in reducing waste and extending the lifecycle of products. Companies in various industries are redesigning their products and business models to facilitate repair, reuse, and recycling. For instance, tech companies now offer device refurbishing programs that reduce electronic waste, while clothing brands have established take-back schemes to recycle old garments into new collections.

Innovative financing mechanisms such as green bonds and social impact investing have unlocked new capital for ESG projects. These financial instruments channel investment into renewable energy, sustainable infrastructure, and social enterprise, empowering companies and communities to implement large-scale, impactful initiatives. Innovation in ESG leadership is about rethinking traditional business models, processes, and technologies to align them with sustainable principles. By being open to experimentation, collaboration, and new technologies, purpose-driven leaders can transform challenges into opportunities and create value for both their organizations and society at large.

Purpose-driven leadership holds transformative power in championing ESG initiatives and overcoming challenges. As we recap this journey, it's clear that leaders who embrace purpose at their core can mobilize their organizations to become engines of positive change. By addressing environmental, social, and governance challenges with clarity and conviction, they guide their teams through uncertainty and toward impactful outcomes that benefit not only their businesses but also society and the planet.

This framework encourages leaders to seek continuous growth, impact, and innovation in their ESG efforts. It's not merely about maintaining compliance or mitigating risks but about pursuing ambitious goals that inspire lasting change. As these leaders navigate resource constraints, shifting regulations, and evolving stakeholder expectations, they embody adaptability, vision, and resilience. Looking to the future, we can envision a world where purpose-driven leadership shapes a more sustainable, equitable, and resilient global community. Leaders who commit to this approach will pioneer new business models, create supportive ecosystems, and foster innovation that transcends traditional boundaries. They will build organizations that uplift communities, regenerate ecosystems, and promote fairness, becoming beacons of responsible stewardship.

As they chart this course, leaders can rely on the guidance of the frameworks, case studies, and strategies we've explored to navigate emerging challenges with confidence and creativity. This path will require courage and conviction, but its rewards will be unparalleled: a world where businesses and societies thrive together in balance and harmony.

Case Study of an ESG Success at Orsted

Orsted, a Danish energy company, stands as an inspiring example of how visionary leadership can reshape an organization's future. Once recognized as one of the most fossil fuel-intensive energy companies in Europe, Orsted underwent a remarkable transformation into a global leader in green energy over the span of a decade. This shift was driven by a firm commitment to sustainable practices and a clear vision of contributing positively to the global fight against climate change.

The company's transformation began under Henrik Poulsen, who took over as CEO in 2012. Poulsen led a bold decision to pivot Orsted's focus from fossil fuels to renewable energy, particularly offshore wind power. This significant change wasn't merely a business strategy; it was a response to the increasing global demand for sustainable energy solutions.

Poulsen and his team took decisive actions to achieve this transformation. They started by selling off oil and gas assets to generate the capital necessary for renewable projects. This move also sent a strong message that Orsted was committed to sustainability. The funds from divestment were then reinvested strategically into offshore wind energy projects, allowing the company to expand its wind energy portfolio rapidly and become one of the world's largest offshore wind farm developers.

Innovation played a crucial role in this transformation. Poulsen's leadership emphasized investment in research and development, which improved the efficiency and cost-effectiveness of wind energy. This technological progress made renewable energy competitive with fossil fuels. Beyond technical advancements, Orsted engaged actively with stakeholders, including governments, investors, and environmental groups, aligning its business practices with broader societal goals. This engagement helped Orsted navigate regulatory environments smoothly and garnered public support for its renewable energy projects.

The results of these strategic shifts were transformative. By 2017, Orsted had reduced its carbon emissions by 52% compared to 2006 levels and targeted a 96% reduction by 2023. Financially, the company grew stronger, proving that sustainability can enhance profitability. In 2020, Orsted was recognized as the most sustainable company globally by the Corporate Knights Global 100 index.

Orsted's journey offers several key lessons in ESG leadership. Visionary leadership from top executives is crucial in driving an organization towards sustainability, as Poulsen's example shows. Moreover, Orsted's experience demonstrates that even companies heavily reliant on fossil fuels can successfully pivot to sustainability without compromising profitability. Innovation is vital, as technological progress makes sustainable options increasingly viable and competitive. Transparent communication with stakeholders builds trust and helps manage transitions effectively, reinforcing the company's commitment to its new path. Orsted's remarkable transformation is a testament to the power of purpose-driven leadership in reshaping industries and contributing to global sustainability. Their strategic approach and mindset have provided a valuable blueprint for other organizations seeking to integrate ESG principles deeply into their operations.

Exercise: Identifying ESG Challenges and Developing a Leadership Response

Objective: This exercise aims to guide leaders through the process of identifying key ESG challenges relevant to their industry and organization and developing a strategic response that incorporates clear goals, action plans, and metrics for success.

Step 1: Context Analysis

Start by understanding the unique context in which your organization operates. Consider the following:
- What industry-specific ESG challenges are most pressing?
- What current global, regional, or local sustainability trends impact your organization?
- How are key stakeholders (customers, employees, investors, regulators) influencing ESG priorities?

Step 2: Internal Assessment

Evaluate the organization's current ESG performance by:
- Reviewing recent sustainability or impact reports, if available.
- Conducting internal surveys or focus groups to capture employee insights on current practices.
- Assessing the alignment between existing business strategies and ESG goals.

Step 3: Stakeholder Engagement

Incorporate input from critical stakeholders:
Conduct interviews or surveys with stakeholders, including customers, suppliers, investors, and local communities. Understand their ESG priorities, expectations, and how they perceive your organization's efforts.

Step 4: Identify Priority ESG Challenges

Based on the analysis from Steps 1-3, identify the top ESG challenges for your organization by:
Listing potential issues impacting your industry. Prioritizing them based on potential risks, opportunities, and stakeholder concerns.

Step 5: Develop Strategic Goals

For each priority challenge, define a strategic goal by:
Clearly articulating the desired impact or improvement. Ensuring each goal aligns with the organization's core values and business strategy.

Step 6: Action Plans

Develop specific action plans for each goal, including:
- Key initiatives required to achieve the goal.
- Roles and responsibilities of team members.
- Resources required and potential partnerships.

Step 7: Define Metrics for Success

Establish measurable key performance indicators (KPIs) for each goal by:
- Defining baseline data for comparison.
- Setting short-term and long-term targets.
- Ensuring the KPIs are meaningful, actionable, and aligned with stakeholder expectations.

Step 8: Implementation and Continuous Improvement

Implement the action plans and:
- Monitor progress regularly using the defined metrics.
- Adjust strategies based on outcomes and feedback.
- Engage stakeholders with transparent communication about the progress and challenges.

By following these steps, leaders will create a proactive and strategic response to ESG challenges that aligns with the broader goals of the organization, ensuring meaningful progress and positive impact.

Chapter 12: Envisioning the Future of Purpose-Driven Leadership

In this final chapter, we turn our attention to the challenges and opportunities that lie ahead for purpose-driven leaders. The rapidly evolving global landscape demands a new breed of leadership that not only anticipates emerging trends but actively engages with them. Leaders must navigate the complexities of technological advancements, shifting economic dynamics, and increasing societal expectations while maintaining their commitment to ethical practices and sustainability. The ability to adapt, innovate, and continuously learn will be critical for staying ahead of these challenges and transforming them into opportunities for growth.

Integrating purpose and ESG principles into future leadership models will be paramount in this evolving context. This involves embedding sustainability, ethics, and purpose into the very DNA of organizations. By fostering a culture that prioritizes these values, leaders can ensure long-term resilience and success. Visionary leaders of the future will guide their organizations not just to profitability, but to make meaningful contributions to the world through positive social and environmental impact.

To help readers craft their path forward, a guided exercise will assist in developing a comprehensive long-term leadership plan rooted in purpose and ESG principles. The exercise will involve evaluating current leadership practices, setting future-oriented goals, and outlining clear strategies to achieve these goals while aligning with emerging trends.

Cultivating a culture of purpose and sustainability will require more than just strategic plans; it will require leaders to embody these values personally and mentor the next generation to continue the legacy. By guiding their organizations to value purpose, sustainability, and social responsibility, leaders can inspire their teams and stakeholders to champion these principles together.

Collaboration will also play a pivotal role in shaping the future of purpose-driven leadership. By forging partnerships across industries and sectors, leaders can work collectively to address global challenges that no single entity can solve alone. Cross-sector networks will amplify impact and promote collective action toward sustainability goals. The journey to purpose-driven leadership starts here. The insights and strategies discussed throughout this book provide a framework for shaping a sustainable, ethical, and impactful future. Leaders must now rise to the challenge, armed with a renewed sense of purpose and vision, to embrace their vital role in creating a world where positive impact drives every decision.

As we look to the future of leadership, understanding the evolving challenges and opportunities within global trends is essential for today's leaders. The rapid pace of technological advancement, the shifting dynamics of the global economy, and increasing societal expectations for corporate responsibility all present unique challenges. Leaders must navigate these complexities while upholding the values of sustainability and ethics.

The potential challenges include keeping pace with technological changes that constantly redefine competitive landscapes and managing the increasing scrutiny from stakeholders who demand transparency and accountability in sustainability efforts. Additionally, leaders must tackle the workforce's evolving needs, who seek meaningful engagement in their work and alignment with their personal values.

To stay ahead of these challenges, leaders must embrace a mindset of continuous learning. By committing to personal and organizational growth, leaders can remain agile and informed about the latest developments and best practices in their industries. This learning extends beyond formal education to include learning from peers, emerging market trends, and different cultural perspectives, which can provide insights into innovative practices.

Adaptability is another crucial strategy. In a world where change is the only constant, the ability to pivot and adjust strategies in response to environmental and market dynamics is invaluable. Leaders who foster a culture of adaptability within their organizations encourage resilience and resourcefulness, which are critical for navigating uncertainties.

Innovation, driven by a purpose beyond profit, can lead to significant advancements in product development, operational efficiency, and customer satisfaction. Leaders should champion innovative practices that not only drive business success but also contribute positively to societal and environmental outcomes. This might involve investing in sustainable technologies, developing new business models that prioritize circular economy principles, or implementing systems that enhance resource efficiency.

These strategies, grounded in a commitment to ethical leadership and sustainability, will help leaders not only respond to emerging challenges but also seize the opportunities they bring. By fostering a culture that values continuous learning, adaptability, and innovation, leaders can ensure their organizations are well-equipped to thrive in an ever-changing global landscape.

In envisioning future leadership models, integrating purpose and Environmental, Social, and Governance (ESG) principles must be a priority. Purpose-driven leadership is crucial in a world increasingly defined by complex societal and environmental challenges. This leadership style will be built around a framework that deeply embeds sustainability and ethics into every aspect of an organization.

A clear vision for integrating purpose and ESG principles into leadership involves rethinking traditional business practices. Rather than viewing these elements as separate from core business functions, leaders will weave them into strategic decision-making, operations, and corporate culture. This comprehensive approach ensures that every decision reflects the organization's purpose and its commitment to environmental and social impact.

At the strategic level, purpose and ESG principles will inform long-term goals, driving the organization toward sustainable growth. Leaders will recognize that aligning with these principles isn't just a matter of compliance or corporate social responsibility. Instead, it's about identifying opportunities for innovation, competitive advantage, and stakeholder engagement. They will identify and prioritize issues that matter most to their business and society, shaping strategies that address these challenges proactively. In daily operations, embedding purpose and ESG requires the development of metrics that measure not only financial performance but also the company's social and environmental impact. These metrics will be transparent and guide all business activities, ensuring consistency between stated values and actual practices. Leadership will foster an environment where employees at all levels feel empowered to contribute to sustainability initiatives and where their efforts are recognized and rewarded.

Embedding sustainability and ethics into the DNA of organizations also means cultivating a corporate culture that values inclusivity, transparency, and accountability. Leaders must act as role models, consistently demonstrating ethical behavior and a commitment to ESG principles. By nurturing a culture where these values are lived daily, leaders create a strong foundation for long-term success. Employees will feel more connected to the organization's mission, knowing that their work contributes to a greater purpose.

Purpose-driven leadership that integrates ESG principles will redefine how organizations measure success, placing equal emphasis on people, the planet, and profit. As more organizations adopt this model, the future of leadership will be defined by a holistic approach that ensures sustainable, ethical practices are at the core of every decision, leading to a more resilient and equitable business landscape.

Cultivating a culture that values purpose, sustainability, and social responsibility requires leaders to be intentional and persistent in their efforts. They must articulate a clear vision that places purpose and sustainability at the forefront of the organization's goals. This begins by embedding these values into every layer of the organization, creating a culture where everyone understands and actively contributes to the broader mission.

First, leaders should lead by example, visibly embodying the principles they advocate. Their actions, from strategic decisions to everyday interactions, should reflect a genuine commitment to the organization's purpose and sustainability goals. By modeling these values, they establish credibility and encourage others to follow suit.

Communication is vital. Leaders need to consistently and transparently communicate the organization's goals, achievements, and challenges in sustainability. They should celebrate successes to reinforce positive behaviors and address setbacks constructively, demonstrating that improvement is always possible. When leaders foster open dialogue, employees feel more engaged and are better able to align their daily tasks with the organization's purpose.

Involving employees in sustainability initiatives creates a sense of ownership and accountability. When employees can contribute ideas and take on roles that support these efforts, they become advocates for the cause. Initiatives like volunteer programs, internal workshops, and cross-departmental sustainability teams can help employees feel more connected to the company's mission.

Leaders should also establish mentoring and training programs focused on purpose-driven leadership. By sharing knowledge and fostering an environment that values continuous learning, they ensure that the next generation is equipped with the skills and mindset necessary to carry these principles forward. Emerging leaders can be given opportunities to lead small projects, allowing them to develop their ability to integrate purpose and sustainability into their decision-making.

Recognizing and rewarding behaviors that align with purpose and sustainability goals reinforce the organization's values. This could include performance bonuses, public acknowledgments, or career advancement opportunities. Positive reinforcement helps embed these principles into the organizational culture. Fostering a culture of purpose and sustainability means creating an environment where purpose-driven leadership is nurtured and sustained. Leaders who inspire by example, communicate transparently, empower their teams, and mentor the next generation are well-positioned to shape organizations that can thrive in a world increasingly driven by sustainability and social impact.

Addressing global challenges like climate change, social inequality, and resource scarcity requires concerted efforts that transcend industry lines and sector boundaries. Cross-industry and cross-sector collaboration allow leaders to tackle these complex issues collectively, drawing on diverse expertise, perspectives, and resources. No organization or sector can single-handedly solve these challenges, but by pooling strengths, they can develop holistic and impactful solutions.

Leaders play a crucial role in fostering collaboration by acting as connectors who identify and bring together like-minded organizations. They must actively seek partnerships with entities that share similar values and goals, even if they come from seemingly unrelated industries. This approach often leads to innovative solutions that might not emerge in isolation. For instance, a technology firm and a non-profit environmental organization could combine their capabilities to create new data platforms that promote conservation efforts. Leaders can further support collaboration by encouraging transparency and trust between potential partners. Honest communication about goals, challenges, and expectations builds a foundation for long-term relationships. By emphasizing shared values and mutual benefits, leaders can create a sense of purpose that unites diverse organizations toward a common cause.

One of the critical functions of leaders in this regard is facilitating knowledge exchange. Creating forums, conferences, or working groups where partners can openly share their successes and lessons learned helps break down silos and cultivates a culture of continuous improvement. When organizations openly share their data, research, and insights, it accelerates the progress of the entire network.

To establish and sustain effective partnerships, leaders must be prepared to adapt and evolve. Collective action often requires flexibility and compromise, as partners may have varying priorities or working styles. Leaders should approach these differences with an open mind, focusing on the shared vision and negotiating solutions that respect each party's interests.

Measuring the impact of collaborative efforts is also important. Leaders should work with partners to establish clear objectives and metrics to assess progress. By monitoring these metrics, they can celebrate successes and make data-driven adjustments when necessary, ensuring that partnerships remain impactful and aligned with broader sustainability goals.

In the end, leaders who champion collaboration and build strong networks create ecosystems that can achieve significant change. They help align diverse sectors toward a sustainable future, demonstrating that purposeful, collective action is the key to solving global challenges. Leaders are uniquely positioned to shape a future where ethical, sustainable, and purpose-driven practices form the foundation of their organizations. By taking proactive steps today, leaders can ensure that their companies navigate the challenges and opportunities of the future with integrity and resilience.

The first step is embedding these principles into the organization's core values and mission. Leaders should articulate a clear vision that prioritizes social and environmental responsibility, emphasizing that the success of the business is intrinsically linked to its impact on the world. When these values are established at the highest level, they become ingrained in every aspect of the organization, influencing decision-making, operations, and stakeholder interactions.

To operationalize this vision, leaders need to set measurable goals that align with their ethical and sustainable objectives. These goals should be ambitious yet achievable, demonstrating the organization's commitment while providing a roadmap for tangible progress. This requires developing a robust strategy that integrates purpose and sustainability into the business model. Whether it's through adopting renewable energy, promoting fair labor practices, or supporting local communities, leaders should identify specific initiatives that align with their goals. Leaders also play a crucial role in building a culture that supports these practices. They must lead by example, embodying the principles they advocate for and recognizing and rewarding employees who contribute to these objectives. This fosters a sense of purpose within the organization, motivating employees to contribute to the broader mission.

Another essential step is stakeholder engagement. Leaders should actively listen to and collaborate with employees, customers, investors, and partners to understand their perspectives on ethical and sustainable practices. This engagement can reveal valuable insights that shape the organization's strategy and strengthen its relationships. It also promotes transparency and trust, which are fundamental for long-term success.

Leaders should continuously seek to innovate and improve their approaches to sustainability and ethics. This requires staying informed about emerging trends, technological advances, and new regulations that may impact their industry. By fostering a culture of continuous learning and adaptability, leaders can position their organizations to remain at the forefront of purpose-driven leadership. They must recognize that ethical, sustainable practices are no longer just ideals but strategic imperatives. By taking these proactive steps, they will ensure that their organizations are not only future-proof but also powerful catalysts for positive change. Their commitment to these values will help build a future where purpose-driven leadership guides businesses towards a sustainable, equitable, and prosperous world.

The journey of purpose-driven leadership, as we've explored in this book, has shown how vital it is for leaders to steer their organizations with a clear sense of purpose and a firm commitment to sustainability, ethics, and social responsibility. In today's interconnected world, the challenges are immense—environmental crises, social inequality, and economic instability require leaders to go beyond traditional business metrics and focus on long-term impact. The importance of purpose-driven leadership lies in its ability to transform these challenges into opportunities for meaningful change. By grounding their actions in a robust framework that aligns organizational goals with ESG principles, leaders can chart a sustainable path forward. They can foster inclusive, innovative cultures that attract top talent, drive customer loyalty, and earn stakeholder trust. They can also contribute positively to their communities, the environment, and society at large.

But the journey doesn't end here. This is a call to action for leaders to fully embrace their unique roles as catalysts for change. You have the insights and strategies to integrate purpose into your decision-making processes, build resilient cultures, and communicate your impact with clarity and authenticity. Your leadership can inspire teams, mobilize partners, and influence the market to follow suit. As you continue your journey, remember that purpose-driven leadership is a continuous practice, not a one-time achievement. Keep learning, adapting, and refining your approach. Seek out opportunities for collaboration and never underestimate the power of your vision. By leading with purpose and vision, you'll help shape a future where organizations prioritize sustainable success and positive impact, setting a standard that will inspire generations to come.

Exercise: Developing a Long-Term Leadership Plan

Begin by reflecting on your current leadership practices and your organization's present strategies. Consider the following questions:

- How do current practices align with purpose-driven and ESG principles?
- What strengths and weaknesses can you identify in the existing strategy?
- What are the existing initiatives that promote sustainability, ethics, and social responsibility?

Based on your assessment, set clear, actionable goals that reflect the principles of purpose-driven leadership:

- What long-term impact do you envision for your organization?
- How can you contribute to the advancement of social, environmental, and economic sustainability?
- How will these goals reflect emerging global trends and challenges?

Create a strategic roadmap that outlines the steps required to achieve these goals. Consider the following:

- What policies or practices need to change to align with your goals?
- How will you ensure all employees and stakeholders are engaged and supportive of these changes?
- What partnerships and resources will you need to realize these goals?

Develop a plan to implement your strategy and measure progress over time:

- What key performance indicators will you use to track progress?
- How will you incorporate feedback and refine your approach?

- How will you communicate progress to stakeholders and ensure accountability?

Recognize that leadership is an evolving practice:

- How will you foster a culture of continuous learning and adaptation?
- What mechanisms will you implement to encourage innovation in leadership practices?
- How will you ensure that your strategy remains aligned with emerging trends?

By engaging in this exercise, you'll create a dynamic long-term leadership plan that integrates purpose and ESG principles, positioning you to guide your organization through future challenges and opportunities.

www.ingramcontent.com/pod-product-compliance
Lightning Source LLC
Chambersburg PA
CBHW071159240526
45470CB00017B/431